Finding Lindy

Melinda Small

Published by Mansfield Anderson Publishers
Printed in the United States of America
ISBN: 979-8-9873155-7-6

DEDICATION

I extend my heartfelt gratitude to those whose unwavering support and encouragement propelled me through the journey of writing and publishing this book. Their contributions have not only given me the courage but have also been instrumental in making this endeavor a reality.

Foremost, I express my deepest thanks to Christina, my daughter-in-law. What began as a birthday gift—a subscription to write a legacy book—evolved into a transformative project of healing and personal growth.

To my husband, whose unconditional support has been a constant throughout the chapters of my life, I am truly blessed. With each "143, I love you," his encouragement has been a source of immeasurable strength.

Special recognition goes to my children, Ryan, Chelsey, and Ashley, whose unwavering support and understanding sustained my motivation during the countless hours devoted to this project. Their belief in me has been a driving force. To my mom, thank you for always loving me, for being the first person to believe in me.

This published book is a culmination of Melissa Mansfield's guidance and feedback. Her keen insights and constructive critiques were pivotal in shaping the final product.

Finally, a heartfelt thank you to the readers whose engagement and interest inspire me without judgment, who encouraged me to accept my authentic self.

Thank you all for being integral to this transformative journey.

CONTENTS

ME

Me I've discovered that I wear many masks. At times, I exude boldness, seizing life with unwavering confidence. Other moments find me retreating into the shadows, embracing my inner shy spirit. There are days I stand tall, bravely facing challenges head-on, and others where fear holds me in its tender grip. My story is a testament to the ever-evolving journey of self-discovery. It's the chronicle of my growth, a testament to the relentless pursuit of authenticity. Each twist and turn, every stumble and triumph, they all form the intricate path that leads me closer to my true essence. I've learned to embrace the bold, the shy, the brave, and the scared. They are not contradictions, but rather harmonious notes in the symphony of my existence. The writing of my story has caused pain, stress, and laughter as I've journaled to a profound sense of peace. If tomorrow were to be my last, I would hope that you'd rejoice, for my life has been a vibrant, kaleidoscopic journey. Yet, if fate grants me another sixty years, I ask that you celebrate alongside me. Rejoice in the love I've given, the wisdom I've gained, and the countless lessons etched into the fabric of my being. For in the end, it's not the length of our journey, but the depth of our experiences that defines us. And I am determined to savor every moment, to dance through life's ever-shifting tides, and to leave a legacy of love and acceptance in my wake.

DAD

Dad was a plumber, a carpenter...a jack of trade. "Lindy, get ready, you're coming with me to work today." Dad tells me in a joyful voice. "See that metal, that's called copper. Watch your step, find all you can in this pile and put it in the bucket." I did as Dad asked. After what felt like hours to a child, Dad yelled, "Get your bucket. This copper will sell for about 5 cents a pound; however, you are going to ask the man for 6 cents. Got it Lindy?" With wide eyes and some nerves my 7-year-old self-asked "Will you pay me 6 cents a pound?" And of course, he did. This was my first lesson in negotiating, taught by Dad. He told everyone the story! He was so proud. "Yup, that's my pride and joy," he would say. The day I was born, Dad purchased the land and the small home in Millinocket, the Pines. It was home for the first 5 years of life. This home was Dad's labor of love and mom's favorite place to be. I loved crawling about to find dad on his latest project. To me dad was superhuman and he proved it on the day he jumped from the roof to the basement. I had fallen from the main floor to the open basement. No stairs to interrupt the fall! Mom's screams told Dad he was needed, and he jumped to retrieve his baby girl. I don't recall the fall. I was too young. I was also too young to know they had lost their first child; baby Lori had died weeks after birth. I can only assume it brought horrible memories as they rushed me to the hospital. It's a miracle mom said over and over for years, a small cut on the top of the head was my only injury. "Lindy, come here we need to talk with you" I believe this conversation to be my earliest memory in life. There is something about grief that stays in the mind. Mom and Dad on the sofa and I on the foot stool. "Mommy and Daddy need to sell the house, we are moving. I remember the tears, my pleading "no, please mommy and daddy. I want to stay here." But that was not possible. Many years later, I found myself longing to see this home, if only for the last time. " Hello, I am Lindy Small, I was Lindy Morrison, and my dad built this home. Would you be so kind as to let me see it? I would love to know if my memories are accurate." It was a small town and the homeowner said "Lindy, I knew you as a baby. I knew your dad and your mom." Knew! The words were a reminder, I was in a small town and she was aware I was in it to mourn moms death. In fact, I was still mourning dad's death from years past. There is something about the passing of the last parent that floods memories! Come in, I have things to show you. How could it be after all these years!" KLM on the homemade closet doors were Dad's initials, (Kenneth Lewis Morrison), next to my first year's height chart. I wanted that door, I wanted to buy it, yet I remained quiet and grateful for the tour. I resisted the urge to ask her if I could have the closet door. For many years after, I wondered if she would have sold it to me. I looked to the living room and in my mind's eye, I could see mom and dad on the couch, me on the footstool as they told me we were moving. It wasn't just the home I would yearn for. What will happen to Clara, Sharon, and Linda (aka, Bunny, Sharon, and Dee Dee to me)? My cousins had become my sisters through foster care. We shared rooms and laughter. Dad had taken the billiards room to make it another bedroom. Two boys and four girls required more space. My cousins/sisters watched over me as the baby in the family. I felt loved and protected. However, Dad was struggling as a self-employed carpenter/plumber. Change would be good, a job offer was accepted in Woodland, Maine, they explained to me as I cried. Our foster sisters/cousins would not be coming with us. I cried as much for them as I did for the security of my home. Life in Woodland didn't provide the change mom and dad were seeking. It wasn't long before Mom was calling Dad's workplace, "Kenny isn't feeling well today and will not be able to work" No one ever says the truth about such things. The calling in to dad's work was my first lesson is keeping family secrets. Children of alcoholics learn this quickly. Just a few short years later, we were moving our mobile home from Woodland back to Millinocket, Kelly's Mobile Home Park was the start of a new chapter.

THE APARTMENT

The Apartment Every action, it seemed, had a reaction. Our apartment was a testament to the consequences of a series of unfortunate decisions, leaving us financially strained and in desperate need of a place to call home. With scant resources, Mom and Dad stumbled upon what would become our sanctuary on Main Street.

It was hardly more than the back corner of my uncle's insurance agency, but with Dad's carpentry skills, it transformed into our apartment, albeit unfinished. It provided us with a roof, but not much else. The scent of old cigarettes and stale beer seemed permanently etched into the walls. It mingled with the worn second-hand furniture and dilapidated kitchen appliances. I should have been grateful for shelter, especially after our stint in a cramped camper with Mom and Scott. I couldn't recount how we got there or for how long we stayed. Every night, as darkness closed in, I cried, and Mom reassured me, saying "it's temporary." The absence of electricity stretched the nights into long, ominous hours. Yet, I couldn't summon gratitude regarding my new home. I despised that apartment. "Kenny, we'll all burn one night." I overheard Mom's voice, a blend of frustration and fear, even though I knew Dad had already succumbed to sleep. Her nightly ritual involved plucking cigarette butts off the blanket. This evening, one ignited. I sprang from bed, driven to ensure the flame was smothered. "Lindy, it's fine, go back to bed," Mom urged. Another night of fitful sleep or nightmarish visions awaited me. The apartment's meager furnishings were stark reminders of our financial straits. The following day, a knock echoed, but no one stood at the door when I answered. On the stoop, a box of Thanksgiving provisions, accompanied by two small Golden Books, awaited me. I was annoyed. "MOM, Golden Books really? I'm not four!" I lamented. Mom gently reminded me to be thankful, as the kind soul who left the box had no inkling of my age. I heard her say, "It's lovely, but I'm not quite sure how to cook a turkey without an oven door." Just across the street stood a bowling alley and a furniture store. After school, I mustered the courage to approach the owner. "Hello, I'm Lindy. Are there any job openings? I want to buy my mom a new stove." He was gracious and assigned me the tasks of dusting and vacuuming. At twelve, I had my first job. I worked diligently for an hour after school every day. "Mom, I earned some money. Can you find a stove with an oven door for

$50?" She welled up with joy. I'm sure there was an exchange of "No, I can't accept this money," but she knew I needed to do this, and accepted with gratitude. Brett, the furniture delivery boy, seemed friendly, perhaps trying to put the awkward cleaning girl at ease. I, however, was too shy to understand how to respond. As I was vacuuming one day, Brett playfully teased or flirted—I couldn't discern. In my confusion, I lashed out, whipping him with the vacuum cord. That marked my last day at the furniture store.

DANNY

I don't have many memories of my older brother Sam living at home with us. He charted his own path at a remarkably young age. My other brother, Scott, three years my senior, and I shared little in common. I imagine I was more of a pest to him than anything else. But on this particular day, I needed something he had. "Scott, can I borrow your Aerosmith album?" I asked. "I don't have it, I let Danny Small borrow it," he replied. "Seriously, why did you do that! Who is Danny Small?" I questioned. "He lives in the double-wide trailer in Kelly's Trailer Park," Scott explained. "If I can get it back, can I have it?" I countered, "Sure, if he'll give it to you!" And off I went on my banana bike in search of Danny!

I can't quite explain why I wanted that album. Aerosmith wasn't exactly my usual jam, even at 13. And being still in my shy, awkward phase, it wasn't as if I had a grand plan. But there must have been something about that album that drew me to it, something that I needed badly enough to go after. I found Danny in the driveway, washing his mom's car. "Are you Danny?" I asked. And that's how Danny and I first met. Danny, 15 years old, with a learner's permit, which meant he could drive, but only with a licensed adult in the car. Clearly, that wasn't going to be me. But he'd turn 16 soon and get his license, and that was good enough for us! Danny enjoys recounting the tale of how his friend Kevin eagerly stepped up to be my boyfriend. However, I prefer to fast forward to the part where Kevin swiftly fell out of contention, and Danny skillfully maneuvered his way into becoming my boyfriend. "I can meet you on Main Street," I responded to Danny's offer of a ride. I wasn't eager for Danny to find out about my living situation. His parents' double-wide mobile home looked like a palace to me. Danny had a fondness for the arcade at the bowling alley, and it was right within sight of my family's apartment. We played side by side, me on one flipper, him on the other. Outside, I could hear the commotion. The kids outside the bowling alley were shouting at the drunken man. It took me only seconds to realize. It was Dad. Mom was on one side of the locked door, but that wasn't going to stop him. Danny had no idea what was happening. One moment, I was playing pinball, the next I was keeping my drunken father from entering the apartment. "Leave, leave now, go away!" I commanded. He was inebriated, but he understood my determination. "You're just like your mother," he spat. "Thank you for the compliment," I retorted, "Now leave!" I'll never understand why, but I was the only one Dad didn't physically harm. In fact, I was the only one who could shield someone else from his wrath. And if I wasn't at home… I felt responsible. With my secret out, I could see Danny watching from across the street as I told Mom to unlock the door and watched Dad stumble away. I stepped inside and locked the door behind me. The home phone rang incessantly. "If it's Danny, I'm not here," I instructed Mom. But the next morning, there he was, standing outside this apartment. "Need a ride to school?" he asked. "I didn't want you to know," I admitted. "I already knew, now get in," Danny said. I think I fell in love with him on that day.

I WASN'T THERE

I Wasn't There There's a common saying about the calm preceding a storm, and it couldn't have been more apparent than on the day I discovered my home in shambles. Following my dad's release from prison, there was a fleeting period of tranquility in our lives. However, one day changed all of it. This day remains etched vividly in my memory.

Dad's arrest for drunk driving marked a turning point. His time behind bars was a revelation for me. I can still recall those visits – his remorse, the fervent promises to mend his ways. The letters he sent, now carefully tucked alongside Danny's love note, remain poignant tokens of that period. Whenever possible, Mom and I would make the journey to visit Dad in prison. The influence of attending AA meetings for Dad and Al-Anon sessions for Mom and me played a pivotal role in securing his release. The call to "gather in a circle and share our feelings" often felt like a tedious ritual. Truthfully, I attended to bring a glimmer of happiness to Mom. But that night, her contentment was far from my thoughts. As the council stood to address the group of women and children, the prompt hung in the air, awaiting responses. Mom stood tall, her voice resolute. "I am so proud of him. His battles are real, but he will never cease striving to conquer them." I rarely clashed with Mom; she was my sanctuary. Yet, on this day, I couldn't hold back. "Proud? Seriously, are you going to use the word 'proud' to describe Dad?" My exclamation reverberated through the room. What transpired next at that meeting is a blur, but 'proud' it was, for Mom. And she was also weary. That day etched into my memory, the table was upturned, facing away from the door. This meant swift access to the room, where I found one chair ensnared beneath the table, two strewn on the floor, and one standing upright amidst the shattered beer bottles. Yet, the most harrowing sight was the absence of Mom, usually there to welcome me home from school. In her place was Dad, a tempest of drunken rage. "Where's Mom?" The panic was palpable in my voice. Every day, I walked to the hospital to visit Mom, unless Danny could drop me off before his shift at McDonald's. "Lindy, you don't have to come every day," Mom would insist. "Yes, I do, Mom. "That night, with Dad slumped over the table, unconscious from drink, I took charge. I cleared the broken glass, emptied the ashtrays, and gathered the empty bottles. As I held one of them above his head, a whirlwind of thoughts raced through me. How hard would I need to strike for it to end? What would come after? The screams I heard were my own. I never learned if the overturned table was a result of Dad's violence towards Mom or if he had discovered her suicide attempt. Years later, I mustered the courage to ask Mom. "How could you? Did you think about what would happen to me?" I could ask Mom anything, and without hesitation, she replied, "Honey, when the pain is this deep, you're incapable of thinking of anything else. You just need it to end." Soon, Mom was back from the hospital, and it was a moving day for both of us. I was eager to leave this apartment, to leave Dad behind. "Honey, we need to move quickly, we can't risk being caught," I assumed a social worker was assisting Mom in planning her escape. I supervised the packing of the cupboards. "Take everything, but leave one plate, one cup, one spoon. Dad needs to eat," she advised, her voice steady.

GENEROSITY

The next apartment felt like a sanctuary. It offered more space, even if not an abundance of bedrooms. I was privileged to claim the sole bedroom for myself. Mom rested on the pull-out couch, while Scott's domain, nestled in the dining area, served dual roles. A simple twist and it was a bedroom, a necessity for privacy. The layout allowed for smooth navigation, save for the slight detour through Scott's 'room' to reach the sole bathroom. But, in all other ways, it was perfect. Sunlight streamed through windows, the kitchen boasted a stove, complete with a working oven door. It carried a pleasant, inviting aroma, and most importantly, it was secure with two entry points, offering a shield against unexpected intrusions by Dad. "Keep the downstairs door locked!" became our mantra whenever anyone stepped out. Despite the precautions, Dad found us again, and Mom, ever hopeful, welcomed him back once he was sober. "Would you mind helping Mom with the dishes, Dad? I'm meeting up with friends!" At 17, time with friends was infinitely more appealing than chores. Dad, wise in the art of negotiation, proposed, "Well,

Honey, it's your duty, but I'll do it for 50 cents." "How about 25 cents?" "Deal!" We both chuckled, sharing hugs before I dashed out. "Be good or be good at it!" Mom's parting exhortation echoed down the hall. Dad shot her a wry look, then began to clear the table. Just like that, the specter of drinking had faded, and our home was once again awash with love. $68.19, a sum forever etched in my memory. Having triumphed in my driver's license exam, Dad inquired about the possibility of a car. My parents were not versed in loans or credit, having little experience with either. Yet, they both had cars. It was Danny who understood the intricacies of loans and financial management. "You might need a down payment," Danny advised. I had been earning at McDonald's, but saving hadn't been at the forefront of my plans. Dad opted to share a car with Mom, selling his own to fund my down payment. With the credit union's blessing, I secured a loan. "What do you think of this car?" I inquired of Danny. "That's a two-door Matador," he noted. "It'd suit you well." His endorsement was all I needed. I could have detested the car, yet I trusted his judgment implicitly. The Matador it was. Mom's caution remained with me, "Lindy, never be late with the payment. Promise, Honey, come to me if you can't make it." Dad assured her, "She'll be just fine."

TEARS AND LAUGHTER

Randy's family owned the three-unit apartment building. They resided in the spacious unit with his parents and two younger brothers. Our friendship blossomed in an unexpected way. Randy and I appeared to be an odd pairing - he was younger, our social circles rarely intersected. Yet, day after day, we found ourselves on the front porch, engaged in conversations about everything and nothing. Mom would chime in, "You kids are going to get piles!" (I even had to Google that term as I wrote this and got a good laugh out of it!) We perched on those chilly concrete steps, discussing whatever came to mind, regardless of the weather. If we tucked ourselves into the door frame just right, it afforded us enough seclusion to sneak a smoke without risking getting caught. I even had to keep my smoking habits hidden from Danny. Randy became my lookout, whispering, "Quick, Danny's car is turning the corner!" A swig of Scope and the evidence of my cigarette indulgence was gone, or so I thought.

While I can't recall the specifics of our conversations, I do remember the laughter. Our sense of humor meshed perfectly. I didn't care if people talked if they approved of our friendship. I simply knew I needed the shared laughter of my good friend Randy. Meanwhile, the laughter with Danny was becoming more sporadic. It was my senior year of high school. Danny had graduated two years prior but felt adrift when it came to choosing a career or even just a job. McDonald's seemed to be the only place hiring. The plans he had for working at the mill would have to wait. It was the path most people took — graduate on a Saturday, start at the paper mill on Monday. But times were changing. The fact that we fought, breaking up and getting back together, as teenagers often do, didn't help. "I've enlisted in the Navy," he told me. The words registered, but nothing made sense. "What does that mean? Where will you go?" To this day, Danny sometimes jokes that he joined the Navy to get away from me. I believe there was some truth in that joke, but not on this day. "I signed up for the military. I leave for boot camp soon," he said. Our on-and-off relationship combined with the job shortage in our area had led us here. Danny was leaving. He was leaving me. Danny handled my tears with tenderness. He was resolute as he explained, "You need to find yourself, and I need to do the same. Date other people, figure out if I'm the one." Danny was always self-assured. Steadfast. Purposeful. I don't think he required or even wanted my input on his decision.

People often mistook our relationship dynamics, assuming I was the strong, decisive one, but that was never the case. With his Duster loaded and his cousin in the front seat, Danny waved goodbye and set off for boot camp. As he departed, I walked into my senior year English class, tears streaming down my face.

FRIENDS AND FREEDOM

My friends Kathy, Nancy, and Patty stepped in to fill the gap left by Danny's absence. Most of my days and nights used to revolve around Danny. Exploring girl time was a new adventure I was eager to embark on. Together, we laughed, we partied, and we met boys. If I told you, you had a beautiful body, would you hold it against me?"' I turned to Kathy, puzzled. "Why would I be mad at Greg for asking that?" She chuckled. "I don't think that's what he meant." "Oh, I get it now," I exclaimed. I was still a bit naïve, but I was all about having fun. "If there's fun, she's in it, won't sit still for half a minute." That's the quote under my senior yearbook photo, and I was determined to live up to it with my girls! Greg was a nice guy, very respectful. Kathy, Nancy, and Patty would all pile into my Matador, and off we'd go to find Greg and his friends. They always made sure we knew where to find them. Eventually, Greg and I found ourselves alone without our friends. It was just him and me, dating. I was enjoying this newfound freedom, but I didn't have any long-term plans for a boyfriend. I made that clear to Greg, but he seemed willing to take the chance. I wasn't exactly a party girl, but I was becoming one. The night I got sick in Greg's mother's car felt like the best time to end whatever was beginning between us. I'm sure he and his mother weren't too thrilled about the mess. My embarrassment provided the perfect exit plan! "Hey Lindy, the phone's for you. It's Greg." "Mom, tell him I'm not home!" The calls kept coming, and Mom would say, "Greg, she's not home." Mom had become my wing woman!

THE PACKAGE

Kathy, Nancy, and Patty continued to fill my nights with girl time, cruising around our small town, and plenty of shenanigans that made for endless adventure. Yet, sometimes, simply sitting in the parking lot on Main Street and talking for hours was all the fun we needed. "Lindy, a package arrived for you from Danny, quick, open it!" Mom's excitement matched my own. Every week, a letter went out to Danny, and one returned from him. These letters are still stored and revisited every few years. However, phone calls were the exception while he was in boot camp. I gently tore open the large envelope. Ah, it's Danny's boot camp graduation photo. On the back, a handwritten note. There was a hushed silence as I read each word. "MOM, he wants to marry me!" I could see the tears streaming down her cheeks. "Of course, he does, Honey. He knows how amazing you are." My shenanigans with friends shifted to wedding planning and shopping. My friends didn't even bat an eye when I said, "I am getting married." They all knew my heart still belonged to Danny. Nancy, Kathy, and Patty organized a beautiful bridal shower with

Nancy's mother's help. We giggled like schoolgirls when I opened gifts of lingerie. Well, we were still schoolgirls after all. However, at the tender age of eighteen, I had no life experience to understand what it felt like for my mom. I didn't realize that with each word read on the back of that photo, her life was about to change. I was leaving.

ENGAGED

Mrs. Danny Small, Mrs. Dan Small, Mrs. Melinda Small..."Melinda, Melinda, are you listening?" My teacher's voice jolts me from my daydream. It's my senior year English class, but my thoughts are on wedding planning, or more precisely, on my new name. "I'm sorry," I stammer. "I am getting married!" The teacher chuckles and says, "Well, that would be a distraction." Each week, Danny sent whatever money he could to contribute to the wedding. However, I spent it on dishtowels, pans, and blankets. Our home was going to be perfect! I was young and a bit naive about wedding planning. I needed a dress and a wedding party. And most of all, I needed Dad to be sober for this one day. Mom knew what else I needed. "What about the Elks Lodge for the wedding?" she suggested. "Yes, that's fine," I replied. "Have you talked to the priest?" Mom inquired. "Nope," was my curt response. "Well, Honey, you'll need to do that soon. "I could overhear phone conversations. Mom's employer at the

29

Brookside restaurant offered to get the food at wholesale cost, and her co-workers/waitresses would help plan the buffet. Another was going to make the bridesmaids' dresses. We just needed the fabric. None of that mattered to me. I was going to be Mrs. Danny Small, and I was moving to San Diego! Looking back, I have no idea how Mom and Dad managed to afford the food, even at wholesale prices, or the $100 to rent the Elks Lodge. They never said a word about it. Many years later, I wonder if I adequately expressed my appreciation for it all or was I just daydreaming... about being Mrs. Danny Small. However, the road to becoming Mrs. Danny Small had its bumps! I am not marrying you, take me home!" Danny was home on leave, and we had a lot to do before the wedding - meet with the priest, decorate the Elks Lodge, have a rehearsal, dinner, and shop for rings. I had saved a little money for his wedding band. "Mom, how will I know if I have enough to buy Danny a wedding band?" I asked. S&H green stamps were a line of trading stamps popular in the United States from 1896 until the late 1980s. They were distributed as part of a rewards program, and Mom had books of the stamps. "Honey, you can have these stamps," Mom said. "Try the S&H store in Bangor, they have everything!" Yet here I was, in tears, saying, "I am not marrying you, take me home!" We went to S&H, Service Merchandise, and every jewelry store in the mall. "Pick out whatever you like," Danny said. I didn't want to embarrass him by picking out something he couldn't afford. He was tight-lipped about how much we could spend. No amount of probing revealed the truth. Suddenly, the overwhelming feelings about budgets, gas to drive to San Diego, hotels, and so much more was becoming real. "Take me home, I don't want to get married!" I cried. And he did. We drove in silence as I sobbed. "I don't know how much money you have," I finally confessed. "I don't want you to pick out a ring based on how much money I have," he confessed. "What if I choose one that costs more than what we have?" "I can get credit." "I don't want credit," I sobbed. I didn't know much about money, but I did learn about bankruptcy. Mom's instilled fear to make payments was still very much with me. "I liked the $500.00 set at Zales in the Bangor Mall. It has a wedding band and the engagement ring for me, and it comes with a matching band for you. I have about $100. If I put that towards the set, can we get that one?" Somehow, we found the words to communicate my fears on this day. I don't recall if Danny let me pay the $100, but I do remember flashing my new ring. I was back to writing Mrs. Danny Small!

Melinda Small

MY WEDDING DAY

The day I was married may be the happiest day of my life. It was perfect, even the light rain couldn't damper my spirit.

Maybe I was always a perfectionist or a control freak, but my hair didn't seem like me. "Lindy, what are you doing" mom says. I don't like the way the beautician did my hair, and I was washing it. She laughed. I think as a mom, I would have freaked out had my daughters had done anything I did. But mom just laughed. You had best be hurrying; you are getting married soon.

My soon to be in-laws Linda and Jr. offered a spaghetti dinner at their home the night before as our rehearsal dinner. Then Danny, I and our wedding party went off to the Elks Hall to decorate. Danny laughs as the streamer gets sucked in by the ac fan. "Danny, stop playing" I scold him and laugh all at the same time! I love it when he laughs, I always have!

The day was June 27th, 1980, and just two weeks earlier I was walking down the different aisle…high school graduation! Nothing was going to ruin this day. Not even the call from Debby, Danny's sister. "Hello, I am bringing a guest to the wedding today" That's fine, who is it" I ask. "Oh no you are not!"

Debby and Greg had formed a friendship, and he was her plus 1. I was firm, Debby was pissed. I had no idea what her motive was for wanting to bring Greg with her. They were not dating, and rumors were flooding he didn't want me to marry. But I didn't care what her motive was, he was not coming to the wedding. "Lindy, can we pad that bra" Mom asks. I was flat chested and all 100lbs! There was no way this wedding dress was fitting in the bust area. An off the rack dress didn't come with alterations, but I didn't care. Sure, we can try, I reply! With dad on my left, my bouquet held upside down lol, I hear the wedding song. The church doors open to my walk. Danny is in full military uniform at the church altar. His dress hat tucked under his arm as he stood tall and proud. He would say, "you are always with me, as he found a way to tuck my graduation photo into a plastic sleeve of the hat." I could see my beautiful bridesmaids in rainbow-colored dresses with big sun hats. Danny was waiting for me with his line of blue tuxedo-clad grooms' men. Dad and I walked arm and arm. He was sober and I was on my way to becoming Mrs. Danny Small with each step. It was a perfect day!

NEW CHAPTERS

Our reception was filled with dancing, family, and friends. I knew it would be the last time I would see them for years. There were tears and cheers as we said our goodbyes to our wedding guests. For our first night, I had reserved a room at the local hotel. However, little did we know, Danny's aunt and a few mischievous friends decided to play a prank on us. They sabotaged our hotel room, removing all the light bulbs, leaving the room in complete darkness. As Danny carried me over the threshold, we stumbled over the displaced furniture. But no obstacle was going to deter me from spending our first night together as husband and wife. Danny's aunt mentioned she would be away for a few days, offering us the use of her apartment while we sorted out our moving details. It sounded like a perfect plan, especially considering our limited funds. She had forgotten she'd lent us her apartment and returned home the next night. Despite all this, I didn't let it bother me. There was too much to be done. "Why do you have so much?" Danny asked as he loaded the rented U-Haul. I had bought pillows, blankets, towels, pans, and, of course, my bridal shower gifts. He chuckled and said, "San Diego has shopping centers, I would have taken you shopping." Nevertheless, he packed everything with care, respecting my need to set up our new home. I knew he didn't think dragging a U-Haul with a Matador 3000 miles across the country was the most practical idea, but he never made me feel guilty about it. Looking back, I realize I had a strong need to prepare. The unexpected wasn't my comfort zone. Gradually acquiring home goods in high school was a safe plan. I wanted to create a cozy home! Saving money for it later seemed too risky. Too many things happened in my life that could have derailed my dreams of a cute home. As I looked at Mom, I felt a lump form in my throat. She was proud yet heartbroken at the same time. We hugged for what felt like hours. I embraced Dad too and was grateful that Mom had a sober Dad to lean on. Tears welled up in Danny's eyes as he said, "I'll take good care of her" when I got into the car. I continued to sob as Danny held my hand and drove out of town. He broke the silence with a caring question, "Do you want to stay here? I can come back as soon as possible." "NO," I laughed, "I want to be with you!" There were no doubts in my mind. Mrs. Danny Small was headed to San Diego. Suddenly, we heard the honking of Mom's car as she raced to reach us. Something must be wrong. "Pull over," I asked Danny. Mom was now out of the car and running towards us. "Lindy, you forgot all the wedding gift money!" We all laughed as Danny said, "NO, we can't do goodbyes again! "I watched

Mom from the rear window of the car. She stood on the side of the road, waving until we were out of sight.

Melinda Small

SAN DIEGO

"Wake up, I don't want you to miss this!" Danny and I were eager to get to our new home. He had it all planned out. "If I continue driving all night, we can reach San Diego as the sun is rising, and I want that to be your first view of San Diego!" Danny told me. My head was heavy, struggling against the weight of sleep. But I could see his excitement. Some fresh air would do the trick, so I rolled down the window. "Oh, Danny, I've never seen anything like it!" I gasped. The glow of the city lights still lingered as dawn began to break. It was a breathtaking sight. He said, "Yes, it is nice, but I really wanted the sunrise to be the first view. You'll see it soon, keep looking, we're almost home." Our 3000-mile trip was nearing its end. We pressed on most days to allow more time to set up our home before he had to report for duty. It was a fun trip. We laughed, played car games, talked about our future, and he tolerated my map reading! Danny had already found our apartment, made the down payment, and paid the first month's rent. But it wasn't without sacrifice. He had to part with his beloved Duster, with its custom hand-painted flames, to afford the plane ticket home and the apartment. Even today, he jokes that he traded his sports car for me, and it was a good deal! "Tell me about our apartment," I asked for the umpteenth time, and Danny laughed. He gave me the same answer he always did, "You'll see it soon." We're here," Danny said, "but I need you to stay in the car for a minute. I'll be right back. Don't get out, ok?" "Sure." He could have asked me to do anything, and I wouldn't have questioned it. He wasn't gone for long, maybe 3-5 minutes. When he opened my car door, I jumped out like a little girl. "Oh Danny, it's beautiful!" Our 1-bedroom furnished apartment looked like the Ritz to me. Danny was exhausted from nearly 15 hours of driving but said, "Let's unload the U-Haul and then sleep. I don't want to risk your stuff being stolen." Fine with me, I was eager to unpack and begin setting up our home. But Danny said no to my enthusiasm for unpacking, "Later, we need sleep." I found sheets, new blankets, and pillows. I knew my advanced planning was needed! I could hear Danny sleeping, but my mind was too busy. He'd be hungry when he woke up. I remembered the grocery store within walking distance. I slipped out of bed quietly and went out the front door. "Damn, I am not in Kansas anymore," I laughed. I settled on a simple breakfast: juice, milk, and powdered donuts. I counted out the money needed to buy them and thanked the lady. Grocery shopping with Mom had never been a thing, so this seemed overwhelming. But my simple breakfast seemed like the right choice as my pans were still packed. I walked back to the apartment. Shoot, which one was it? It's upstairs, to the left. I remembered...DAMN IT, I forgot the key! One of my neighbors told me there was a property manager on-site who would unlock the door. That's a good plan. I don't want to wake Danny. The property manager told me there was a charge for unlocking the door. "Thank you, but I am not comfortable spending any money right now." As I left, he smiled and said, "I'll give you this time free." "Shh, do it quietly," I asked the property manager. "I don't want to wake him." I'll tell Danny about this adventure later, I decided, as I quietly began unpacking. Where are the wedding dishes? I wanted to use the good stuff for the milk and donuts! Soon Danny was stirring, "Don't get out of bed!" Danny was served his first breakfast in bed by his wife! In fact, it became one of my favorite ways to spoil him. Many years later, I asked him why I had to stay in the car. He told me, "California had roaches, I used a pest bomb before I left to get married. I wanted to be sure it was clean without evidence of roaches."

Melinda Small

BECOMING THE NEW ME

"Babe, I don't think we'll have enough money for groceries."
Living on a military paycheck was no easy feat. Danny and I were
learning the ropes of adult life quickly. It was just him and me,
and together we navigated our way. "Let's walk down to the
pawn shop. We can sell my small black and white TV," he
suggested. An hour later, we had $50.00 in cash. "I have a plan,"
I declared. "We'll be rich." "What's the plan?" he asked. "I'll
write a best-selling book on how to feed two people for a month
on $50.00!" We both laughed. "I get paid next week; we'll be
fine," he assured me. It was a week-to-week budget, but we made
it work. Extra money went towards adventures! "Las Vegas is
just 6 hours away, get in, I'll take you to Vegas!" "Tijuana is just
30 minutes away; get in, I'll take you to Mexico!" "Today is
Balboa Park and roller skating!" The list went on and on. I never
had to plan anything other than sandwiches. I loved that every
day Danny had off from work was an adventure day. Many times,
we slept in the car and packed our own lunch, but none of that
mattered. "Babe, I can get a job, the extra money will be good.
There's a McDonald's within walking distance." Danny would

assure me, "I can take care of us." However, I wanted to help. I landed the job at McDonald's, of course; I had plenty of experience. But it wasn't long before I was seeking something different. Unfortunately, dealing with harassment in 1980 was a whole different ball game. My manager's inappropriate requests made my choice clear: endure it or leave. I left! The local 7-11 was hiring, and the hours would sync up better with Danny's schedule. But I got bored there, so when a friend told me I could bag groceries at Safeway for $7.00 an hour, I was all in! $7.00 was more than I had ever made. "It's a union job," they explained to me. "Danny, what's a union job?" He did his best to explain. I learned enough to be bored. I had two responsibilities at Safeway: dispose of the day-old bread each morning before 6 a.m. and bag groceries to carry out to cars. Danny didn't like me walking to work in the early mornings. Most days, he got up early to drive me. However, on nights he worked late, he told me to take the car and he would walk to get it when he woke. Rick was my manager. "Rick, why do I have to rip the plastic off the bread bags before trashing it? The homeless are out there; can I give it to them?" Rick told me, "For the safety of all, it needs to be torn open and placed in the dumpster." Each morning, I would rip the plastic as I was taught and toss it in the dumpster with homeless people waiting to see the gifts of the day. The dumpster had a platform around it. I simply tossed while the homeless tried to reach. "Rick, I have another question. I was taught to rip the plastic bag completely open. Are there any rules that say how big the rip needs to be?" "No, Lindy," he laughed and said, "You're a good person." I was so eager to get to work each day to see how the day-old bread was stocked. My pitch was getting good; I could land the bread right next to a person without any slices spilling out. Mom and Dad had taught me generosity, and my amazing husband was proud of me!

Melinda Small

MY FAVORITE TEACHER

"Lindy, you need to stop this. Being late for work in the military is no joke," Danny scolded as he crawled into bed. It had become a routine - the alarm would go off, he'd shower, and I'd slip into my bridal shower lingerie. He'd end up running late. Eventually, he wisened up and started setting the alarm earlier. "You should drive me to work today," Danny suggested. "You know I can't handle the traffic; it's too overwhelming for me," I defended. "If you learn to navigate it, you could meet me for lunch any day you're not working. We could sit at the stone wall overlooking the bay," Danny persisted. The idea was tempting. Driving to the grocery store for work was only a mile away, but the military base was an entirely different prospect! "I would love that, but I'm too scared," I confessed. Before long, Danny was back from work. "Let's go," he said. "Where are we going?" I asked. "We're going to the mall," he replied. As we walked around, our only purchase was warm pretzels to share. The next morning, Danny said, "Get up, you're taking me to work today. It's only two lanes, and it's a straight shot. You got this." He coached. I listened to his instructions intently. He was right; it wasn't as bad as I thought. He leaned over to kiss me goodbye and placed something in my hand. "What's this?" I asked. "I got a credit card; it has a $500.00 limit. Follow the directions I showed you yesterday and go back to the mall. Go spend this on whatever you want!" "What if I get lost? What if I get into an accident?" Danny always assured me, "If I thought that would happen, I wouldn't want you to do it. Now go have fun and pick me up after work," he said as he kissed me again and shut the door. I drove cautiously, like a 90-year-old, but I made it. I was so proud; I couldn't wait to tell him. I didn't make a single purchase; there was nothing I needed. I only wanted to get back home to make dinner and pick him up. "Where are your packages?" he asked. "I really did do it; I just didn't need anything," I assured him. Danny believed me - he had no reason not to. I have never lied to him, nor would I. After dinner, we were back at the mall. "I like this, try it on," he said. And that is how it started. My journey to confidence.

MY FIRST COUCH

"Danny, stop the car, did you see that?" I exclaimed, unable to contain my excitement. I knew he despised my outbursts while driving, but I couldn't let him miss it. "See WHAT?" he replied in a panic. "That shop. They make couches." I replied, still bubbling with enthusiasm. "You have a couch," he said, his annoyance evident." No, it's a rented one. Can I at least look?" I pleaded, knowing he couldn't refuse. Inside the shop, the salesperson explained, "You pick out a fabric and then choose a sofa style you like. We'll deliver in one month. "It might not have meant much to some, but to me, it felt magical. "Oh, I adored that blue flowered fabric!" Danny reminded me, "We have an apartment, there's no room for another couch." "Can the property manager put the one that comes with the apartment in storage?" I asked eagerly. "You can ask him," Danny replied, giving me the green light. The next day, while we were having dinner, Danny asked, "Why the pouting face?" "The property manager said we can't move the couch out of the apartment." "Does that mean we're moving?" Danny inquired. It hadn't occurred to me, but we could move! And so began my hunt for a new apartment. "Danny, I found one with a pool, near the beach! Want to see it?" "No, that's fine, I trust you," he said. Little did he know what a big mistake that was! Boxes packed and our new sofa ready to be delivered, I arrived at the office. "Hello," I spoke through the security system. "I need to check the move-in details for tomorrow, how do I get a key?" "What's your name?" The familiar office manager was absent, replaced by a stern older lady who claimed to be in charge. "Melinda Small," I said, "I'm sorry, we have no record of you," she stated. After a pause, she buzzed the door open. "Come in." She continued, "The office assistant had an emergency. Maybe she didn't process your paperwork. Did you pay?" "No, I thought I paid on the move-in day. She told me tomorrow was my move-in date," I explained, tears welling up. "Can I pay today?" "We don't have any open apartments!" The tears flowed freely now, but I tried not to further embarrass myself. She considered for a moment. "Hold on," she said, leaving the room. When she returned, she told me, "The owner of the building is on his way. Don't leave. "In walked a businessman with kind eyes. "I hear you have a problem," he stated." Yes, sir, I do," I replied. "Tell me about yourself." "Well, I work at Safeway as a grocery bagger, and my husband is an E-3 in the Navy." "You're quite young for a military spouse," he noted. "I'm 18," I said proudly. "Well, darling, that's a problem. Only E-5 and above are approved to live here," he informed me. My face drained of color. "Okay, thank you," I managed to say, standing to leave. "Hold on," he said firmly. "Sit down." He turned to the manager and said, "Put her in the two-bedroom on the first floor overlooking the beach. "Sir, I can't afford a two-bedroom," I stammered. "Yes, you can. I'll give it to you rent-free, but you must vacuum the hallways and collect rent payments on weekends." The manager led me to the apartment. "Will this do?" she asked. I spotted the couch. "Yes, ma'am, but I have a couch arriving tomorrow." "I'll have this one moved to storage," she assured me. I couldn't believe my luck. I returned to the office to thank the businessman. "I promise I'll do a good job. "He extended his hand, and I grasped it in what I believe was my first-ever handshake. He may not have been a constant presence, but every time I saw him, he'd ask how I was doing. In some strange way, I felt protected by him, and I trusted him implicitly.

People come into our lives at different times to teach us important lessons. He taught me to trust. As I walked back to our apartment, I eagerly awaited Danny's return. With just a few boxes and our wedding gifts, moving a few blocks was a breeze. "Danny don't be mad at me," I began, though he rarely ever got angry. "I made a mistake, but I fixed it. You won't believe how." However, vacuuming the 2 story units was more of a challenge than I expected and our time at apartment 2 was less than 1 year. "Lindy, you can't vacuum the halls of this building. It's too big, and you can't carry the vacuum up the stairs!" "I'll do it!" he declared, much to my surprise. I knew he loathed vacuuming two floors each weekend, but he was willing to help. " Babe, find a new apartment. This time, I'll help," he offered. "But it looks like we need a bed and a kitchen table!" Three apartments in two years, all because of a couch! LOL!

GOODBYE SAN DIEGO

As my time in San Diego drew to a close, I couldn't help but feel the weight of its significance. These years held a richness that I often find myself trying to put into words. I'd turn to Dan and ask, half in jest, "Could we have a do-over for these chapters of our lives?" The truth is, I wouldn't change much. I'd simply relish the chance to experience it all anew. In my rewritten tale of departure, we'd revisit our cherished spots, savoring romantic nights filled with shared memories and intimate moments. Every minute with Dan would be soaked in, treasured like the rarest of gems. However, fate had a different script in mind. Dan's parents, having not visited us before, chose this moment to make the journey before our departure. It altered the narrative significantly. In hindsight, I've come to realize so much about myself. Foremost among the lessons was the recognition of my tendency to put others' needs before my own. When Dan's parents shared their ambitious plan - a 3,000-mile drive with an aging dog and elderly parents flying in from Germany - the courageous response would have been, "No, that won't work for me." "My daughter-in-law embodies this courage. She knows the power of setting boundaries, and our son stands steadfastly by her side. It's a quality I deeply admire in both of them. Yet, it was a skill I lacked, and even if I had possessed it, I suspect Danny would have persuaded me to go along with the flow anyways. I remained silent, despite my inner turmoil and appeals to Danny. Our once-filled apartment was now sparse, blankets and pillows reserved to fashion makeshift sleeping arrangements on the floor. The dog, a silent trespasser in our pet-restricted space, held our deposit in jeopardy. The word "no" felt foreign to me, even though my heart. The cross-country journey back home was stressful, and now it was even more so. By the trip's end, I couldn't help but wonder if everyone secretly wished I'd spoken up. The journey had taken its toll on the elderly grandparents from Germany, and the dog, drooling and uncomfortable, bore the brunt of the 3,000 miles. Inside, I seethed with frustration, desperate for a moment of privacy, a warm shower, and the comfort of a hotel bed. My internal screams fell silent, drowned out by the choices made for me. I can still hear the relentless thumping of oil drilling in Texas, the soundtrack to my restless night of sleep in the cramped camper. It seemed that everything was orchestrated according to others' desires, right down to when and where we ate. I harbored no blame towards anyone but myself. My voice was lost in the cacophony of others' needs, buried beneath the fear of confrontation. And 43 years later, the struggle to put my own needs first persists. The mantra, "When others are happy, I'll be happy," has defined far too many of my years. Our return home brought stormy days for Danny and me. The chapters that followed would challenge us in ways we never anticipated.

Melinda Small

BROKEN

With a settlement for his back injury, Dan found himself suddenly flush with cash. He invested in a mobile home in Medway and a few other things, his intentions as pure as the morning sun. Money coursed through his fingers like quicksilver, yet every expenditure carried a purpose, a dream. Dad, a good man battling the relentless grip of addiction, beamed with pride, offering, "Lindy, you can stay in the trailer as long as you need." Dad was a generous man, and I was blessed to marry one as well. The trailer, though weathered with age, felt like home. Until I realized Mom and Dad were off on their familiar dance. Dad, ensnared by the bottle once more, brought home a Winnebago. Since it was his land, parking it in his driveway felt like a decree, a verdict I dared not contest. "Why? Why now?" I silently questioned myself. "Why did Dad, two years sober, stumble back into the clutches of alcohol the moment I returned home? It had to be me." "Danny, we need to find work," I declared. But Danny, ever the provider, had already made up his mind. "I'll return to McDonald's until the mill calls me back," he resolved. "And I'll join Mom as a waitress," I added, and so we did. The diner's seats witnessed more idle chatter than bustling service. This waitress wage wouldn't pry me from Dad's trailer. For now, I bid my time, waiting for a better opportunity to unveil itself. Then came Thanksgiving. I adorned the table with my finest dishes, eager to craft a feast for Mom, Dad, Danny, my brother Scott, and his wife. We nestled into the built-in seating, but the scent of stale beer mingled with the aroma of turkey. I strained to ignore it. Earlier that day, I stumbled upon Dad's hidden stash of pills nestled among my bathroom towels. I flushed them all away, watching as cars came and went from our driveway. Dad had money, and people had painkillers. I had gotten rid of them, knowing confrontation loomed. When Dad spilled his soda and slurred his apologies, I found my voice. "Get out. Leave!" I commanded. Mom worked to quell the tension, but a new Lindy emerged, defiant. "Get out! You ruin everything, Dad!" He mumbled about ownership and legacy as he stumbled away. "Why did I return here? I despise Millinocket," I muttered. Resentment pulsed in my veins. Change was inevitable, and I knew it. But for now, I monitored Dad. He could be gone come morning. Knock, knock. "Dad, are you awake?" I whispered, his snores confirming his slumber. The Winnebago bore the stench of regret, mingled with cigarette smoke and stale beer. There, on the table, lay remnants of my childhood - torn school pictures. I collected them, tears tracing silent paths down my cheeks. They were mine now. Exiting the Winnebago, I cradled my fragile treasures. Those photos, once cherished, now bore scars of my history. Someday, my children will unearth them, and I wonder, how will they interpret these remnants of my secrets?

Melinda Small

MORE THAN A NEW JOB

Maybe Frank saw something in me, some potential waiting to be honed. Perhaps he sensed a malleability, a raw capability. Whatever it was, he took a gamble on me. The last time I'd ventured into the professional job market was back in San Diego. The office manager's voice was firm but encouraging, "Please type this letter. You'll be timed, and remember, no peeking at the keys, just focus on the paper." I felt confident, I could type! I pressed each key with care, mirroring the characters on the page. "Time's up," she declared. I looked down, only to find my fingers had strayed. Cheeks flushed; I handed over my attempt. "Thank you for your time. That will be all," she dismissed me. As I left, I couldn't shake the feeling of inadequacy. "I didn't do well. She won't be calling me back," I confided in Danny. Bagging groceries suddenly seemed like the perfect fit. But here I was, applying for a bank teller position. Borrowing Mom's knee-length spring coat, I hoped it lent an air of maturity and professionalism. "Mindy, can you start training next week?" Frank, the loan officer, offered me a lifeline. "Yes, thank you. Where do I go for training?" I asked. "You'll start in the Bangor office and then join us here in Millinocket," he explained. I could handle the drive to Bangor, I thought. No more waitressing for me! I never mustered the courage to correct him about my name. By the time I reached training, my nameplate proudly read "MINDY SMALL." I decided not to make a fuss; Mindy it would be! With Danny at the mill and me at the bank, we could finally move out of Dad's trailer and into one of our own. Owning land was a distant dream, so Kelly's Mobile Home Park became our reality, just a stone's throw from Danny's parents' double wide. Packing Danny's lunch and a salad for myself, I prepared for my first day of training. Nerves danced in my stomach. What if there was another typing test? I dreaded the thought. I left earlier than necessary, determined not to be late. "Wait here, you're quite early," the receptionist instructed. "We'll check you in soon." I stood there awkwardly in Mom's coat, grateful that it had at least gotten me this far. "Are you new here?" a voice broke through my anxious reverie. "I'm in training for a few days, then I'll be at the Millinocket branch," I replied, trying to sound confident. "You can hang your coat here," he offered. I relinquished Mom's coat, and he hung it up with a kind smile. Small talk filled the air as I waited for my trainer. The all-glass room with its imposing table made my head spin. "Please introduce yourself and tell us about your work history," the trainer instructed. Was it the windows or my nerves? I needed to steady myself. "Hello, I'm Melinda Small. I recently moved from San Diego, where I

FINDING LINDY

worked as a bagger!" I cringed inwardly at my choice of words, but I was determined to learn and prove myself. The morning passed quickly, and I found myself engrossed in the new information. Lunchtime came, and I found a secluded table in the corner, hoping to hide my nerves. Eating in front of strangers was a new level of anxiety for me. Just as I thought I was in the clear, I spotted Bill from the morning, heading in my direction. Don't make eye contact, maybe he won't see me, I thought. "Mind if I join you?" he asked. I picked at my salad, too nervous to eat properly. Bill, the assistant loan manager, put me at ease with his easy conversation. I excused myself to return to training, relieved but slightly mortified when he gently corrected my direction. "How's training going?" Bill checked on me occasionally, offering encouragement and reassurance. I was in Bangor for just a few more days before starting my shifts in Millinocket. I learned my new role swiftly. Millie, the lead trainer at the Millinocket branch, was tall, elegant, and serious. Yet, she seemed to take a liking to me. "Try this on," she said one day, presenting me with a one-piece jumpsuit. "You'll need heels," she advised. I couldn't hide my excitement - I had heels! Millie's clothing surpassed my entire budget but wearing those 'good things' felt transformative. With newfound confidence, I embraced my role. Customers would wait just to be served by me. One elderly man, a regular in my line, once crafted a flower from one-dollar bills. He explained that his wife had passed, and he was moving to live with his son. Before he left, he wanted to thank me for my kindness. "I can't accept money," I insisted. He was crestfallen, unable to fathom my refusal. "Wait here," I implored, clutching the floral creation as I approached Frank's office. I explained the gesture and asked if I could accept it. Frank agreed, and I decided to donate the money, ensuring I stayed in the clear. A month later, Frank announced the arrival of an assistant manager, Bill Smith. It struck me - this was the same Bill I'd met during training in Bangor.

GOODBYE DAD

Writing this story is never easy. Many of them aren't. But this one, this one feels like trying to hold back a tide of emotions. It's challenging because, unlike most hurts in life, this one was self-inflicted. Bill seamlessly transitioned into his new role, becoming a beloved member of the team. It wasn't surprising. Bill was diligent and charismatic. Meanwhile, my father was in the hospital. It was a familiar scene; he'd been admitted before. This time, however, would forever haunt me. Seeing him wheeled out of X-ray, so frail and vulnerable, left an indelible mark. At 52, his liver was failing, and his body was a mere 86 pounds of weakness and malnourishment. Yet, even in that moment, I clung to the belief that Dad would somehow bounce back. He always did. I sat by his side for hours, holding his hand. Annoyance, sadness, and anger swirled within me. How could such a good man burden so many with his illness? Eventually, my mother arrived at the hospital. Relief washed over me; she'd take over now. Despite their divorce, she was a steadfast presence. "Mom, I need to leave," I confessed. She understood the personal turmoil I grappled with, even as we faced Dad's struggle. "Where will you go?" she inquired. "I'm going to spend the night in a Bangor hotel. I need time to think about Bill, about Danny, about what I need to do." It felt like a sanctuary, knowing both Bill and Dan would be in Millinocket. I assured Mom, I'd keep her posted on which hotel I chose. And I did. "Hi Mom, I'm settled in at the hotel. Here's the number if you need to reach me." In those days, there were no cell phones, no tracking devices. She confided that dad was arguing with her about something. To avoid the tension, she'd gone home. Dad seemed to be rallying, or so I believed, until the phone rang an hour later. "Lindy, Dad has passed. "The words hung heavy in the air. A maelstrom of emotions engulfed me. Joy mixed with sorrow, worry for Mom, and the unmistakable ache in her voice. I hung up the phone and sank to my knees. "Please, Lord, welcome this gentle soul. Restore his body and spirit. Daddy, watch over Mom. Most of all, find peace."

FINDING ME

I can't tell when or how it happened. Maybe it started the day I handed Bill my coat. Maybe it started the day he walked into the Millinocket office as the new assistant manager. Maybe it happened simply because it became part of my journey. I don't know, but I do know, it wasn't planned. At least not by me. I don't think Bill planned it either. However, I could sense the chemistry between Bill and me. I would catch him looking at me and then smile when he was caught. He was confident and handsome. The entire thing confused me. I was married. I didn't feel as if I was attractive. I dismissed the small signs to my imagination. I dismissed his attention as unreasonable. He could get a woman easily; he didn't want me! However, it appeared he did. I don't remember telling Danny. I am sure I've blocked this out, yet I must have. I do remember packing my things as I moved out of our mobile home and into my own apartment. I opened up to Mom about my troubles, my confusion over what I wanted. "Mom, I don't know what to do?" I finally confess. There was no shame with Mom. She advised me, "Danny is a good man." "I know, it makes this all harder." I replied. We talked for a few more hours. I told her, "I need to go for a walk." "I know you do; be careful of the direction you walk in and give me a hug." I loved mom's advice on this night. She didn't tell me what to do, she encouraged me to find my own way. Mom and Danny were very close. Her support of me to find my own way changed their relationship. It wasn't long before everyone seemed to be involved. Dan's mom and dad met with Bill at McDonalds." Bill, please do not meet with them", I asked. But he did. Danny was steadfast in his love for me. "What are you doing this weekend?" Danny asked. "I'd like to take you on a date." "A date!" I reply. "Yes, a date." He laughs. Danny is a man of few words and lots of action. He always has been. "Lindy are you home" I can hear Danny climbing the stairs to my apartment. "Yes, come in, I am making chop suey." "That smells good," he said. "You hate chop suey" I said, rolling my eyes. Years later Danny told me he thought Bill was in my apartment that night, maybe hiding in a closet. He was not! I chuckled at this, thinking if the shoe was on the other foot, I would have trashed the place to find the woman. Yet, he was patient! "I like chop suey tonight" he said as he passed me a jewelry box. "What's this?" I ask. "Just a little gift I wanted you to have." He smiles. "Danny!" I roll my eyes. Danny's lack of words and our communication issues often leaves me waiting for what comes next. I've learned to just be still, and in time I'll see what he wants or needs. In truth it is hard for me to be still. It brings me back to times of expected trauma. Danny may be a man of action, but he is also a confident, tolerant, patient, and non-confrontational man. When Bill told me "I met with Danny last night," I was shocked! "Good Lord, why would you agree to meet with Danny?" "Why would Danny want to meet with you?" I rattled on! Bill told me very little about the meeting. He left it at "If I can't love you as much as he does, he asked me to let you go." Bill had never told me he loved me. I ran away again another night when it was all too much for me. With Danny and Bill in Millinocket, a runaway to a Bangor hotel to rest my mind seemed like the perfect solution. Again, no cell phones, no tracking devices. I was free to be alone. However, when a man wants a woman, he will find her! The first knock on the door is Bill. Mindy, please open the door. Back in 1983 the hotel would give the room number without question. Bill found my car at the hotel and was knocking on the door. I was shocked and reluctant to allow him into the room. He promised to stay for just a few minutes and wanted to talk to me. He explained he had something to do and would come back later to explain it all. The second knock is from the man who would find me in any hotel in the universe. "Babe, let me in. I am worried about you" Good lord, how will this look if Bill comes back is all I can think about! Danny tells me he wants me to come home. I just want to get out of the hotel before Bill returns. I left a note for Bill with the hotel clerk explaining to Bill that I belong with Danny.

To this day, I don't know if Bill returned to find my note or just me gone! Bill left the Millinocket office soon after.

BECOMING A MOM

"Can this be? Did it happen so fast?" I wondered, gazing at the calendar. In 1984, home pregnancy tests weren't as reliable. Confirmation required a doctor's visit. "Danny, I think I'm pregnant!" We'd only just decided a few months ago that it was time to start our family. Danny, flourishing at the Mill, and I, still at the bank, had our beautiful two-bedroom mobile home. "Seriously? Make a doctor's appointment soon," he advised. And I did. "Yes, Mrs. Small, you are pregnant," the doctor confirmed. "Oh, I need to get home. I want to make a nice dinner and surprise Danny," I rushed out of the doctor's office.

Keeping secrets from Danny was a challenge for me, especially when they were this exciting! I planned it all out. The table would be set just right, using our finest dishes. After he'd relish his favorite meal, I'd tell him. But he saw it the moment he walked through the door. My beaming smile said it all. "You're pregnant, aren't you?" he asked. I ran and jumped into his arms. "You're going to be the best Daddy!" I told him.

A few days later…" Come sit down," Danny said. Danny always had a list of dos and don'ts. "Popcorn is good for the baby," he declared. "And I got a thermometer. You like your baths hot, but too hot isn't good for the baby," he continued. He wasn't kidding. I loved my garden bathtub; every bath was tested for temperature before he carefully took my hand, ensuring I wouldn't slip. "Babe, I think you should be pregnant all the time; your bowling average is increasing." He thought he was quite the comedian; I told Lyla, our bowling partner. "I'm not bowling; my pants don't fit," I told Danny the next week. "Here, you can wear my sweatpants with the elastic waist. I'll take you to Bangor tomorrow for some pregnancy clothes. "My entire pregnancy was wonderful. I never had a day of morning sickness. Danny took wonderful care of me and his pending bundle of joy. "Danny, I want to decorate the baby's room." "Why don't you wait until you give birth? You don't know yet if it's a boy or girl," he suggested. Good Lord, did he forget he married a woman who needed to buy towels and tote them 3,000 miles across the country!" "No, I want to have it ready. I can decorate it yellow. That's good for a baby boy or girl." Danny rarely said no to me, and he didn't on this day either. "Babe, I don't feel well, I am having horrible cramps," I said, finding myself at the bottom of the bed as he woke up. My labor was hard, compensating for the easy pregnancy. Danny had a weakness around needles. When the doctor started the epidural block, Danny was ready to pass out. Staggering out to the waiting area, his face was pale as a ghost. That alarmed Mom. "Danny, talk to me, is she okay?"

Mom's voice trembled with concern. Danny could not talk! Finally, he found his voice. "Yes, she is just having a hard time. We need to get a second doctor in the room to help," he told Mom. But that did little to reassure her! Our baby was trapped. It was too late for a C-section, and too difficult for a vaginal birth. After far too many hours of labor, fraught with serious complications, the doctor told me, "Do not push; you have to resist the urge. "Exhausted, I nodded off for seconds, then woke up again. Danny was making eye contact. "Honey, we need to do this together, you can't push. Just look at me!" Finally, our baby was born, with the aid of forceps. However, our baby was quiet. I looked at Danny. "Is it a boy?" "It's a boy," he said. "Where is he?" I was eager to hold my baby. "The doctor just needs to check him. Don't worry, he will be fine. Try to rest," he advised. I had been in hard labor for over 20 hours, 14 of which were hard labor hours! "Please bring me the beige dress with the pink trim," I requested. "Make sure the car seat..." Danny stopped me. "I got everything set up. How are you feeling?" "My headache is a little better. I'm just tired. The doctor said I can go home today." I wasn't being entirely honest with myself. I was more than just tired. I was simply eager to go home. Danny dressed Ryan in his new sailor suit, and I slipped into the bathroom to put on my size 3 dress with the pink trim. "Babe, what's wrong?" Danny heard me crying. "My dress doesn't fit. I wanted to look cute for you while you drove us home. "Danny replied, "Babe, open the door." He hugged me. "You are cute. I brought you some maternity pants and a top. You'll be more comfortable in this. He just always seems to know what I need, even when I don't. "With fresh sheets on the bed, a corner folded down, and Ryan's bassinet next to me, Danny had ensured everything was perfect. "You need to rest. Ryan and I are right here; you have nothing to worry about," Danny assured me. But deep down, I knew I was in trouble. Rest wasn't going to fix everything. The doctor explained, "A second epidural was administered in error, Mrs. Small. There's no easy way to tell you this. You have an air gap. As your blood circulates, your brain is sensing the gap. You'll have painful headaches for a while. They will get better." A whisper sounded like a train horn in my head. Lifting my head was impossible. And now, I was hemorrhaging. "Lindy, you're losing too much blood," Danny said. "The doctor told me I would bleed," I replied. "It's too much. You need to go back to the hospital. I'm calling an ambulance." "Please NO, the sound of sirens would be impossible." "Then I need to carry you." "No, Danny please." The thought of uncontrolled movement was too much. "I'll go, but you have to let me crawl to the car. "I crawled for a few feet; the rest became a blur. I knew Danny was carrying me as I rested my head on his chest. "Sit here; I'll be right back," Danny said. I was unable to care for Ryan for the first two weeks of his life. Between Danny and his mom, Ryan's needs were met, and he was loved. I was grateful, yet I was eager to learn my role as his mom. Danny soon walked through the hospital door. "Ryan, meet your Mommy," he said as he gently placed Ryan in my arms. "Mommy, meet Ryan Kenneth Small. "I had held Ryan a few times prior to this day, yet nothing compared to this moment. Dan and I had lots of discussions about what to name our baby boy. However, there was no question… Ryan would be all the wonderful things my father was and wanted to be. His middle name would be in his namesake. Hearing the words, "Mommy, meet Ryan Kenneth Small," filled my heart with joy.

Melinda Small

NOT WHAT I HAD PLANNED

I had left my job at the bank weeks before giving birth, working up until nearly the last day to ensure we had enough savings for me to become a stay-at-home Mom. "Babe do not worry; I make enough money to take care of all of us," Danny reassured me. He didn't hesitate when I told him I wanted to focus on being a homemaker and mom. He earned, and I managed the finances. I knew the budget would be tight, "Babies are expensive," I'd remind him. "I can work overtime anytime you need more, just let me know," Danny replied, ever the supportive partner. I quickly settled into the rhythm of being a full-time homemaker and mom. I relished in this role; a clean home, dinner on the table, happy baby, and romantic nights - it all felt perfect. So, when he was home in the middle of a work shift, I was perplexed. "Why are you home so early?" I asked. "They cut the shift today," was all he said. I sensed a weightiness about him. When he was ready, he would share what was on his mind. Yet, waiting wasn't my strong suit. Over the years, I'd learned to be patient, to not push. When Danny was ready, he'd open up.

Other times, it was a simple, 'You don't need to know,' as a response. Accepting "You don't need to know" took time, even though I knew he wanted to shield me from unnecessary worry. But still, not knowing weighed on me. On this day, I was worried; I knew something wasn't right. Playing with Ryan, Danny broke the news, "There's a layoff at the mill, my timecard is pulled." I struggled to grasp the magnitude. "What does all that mean?" "It means we have no income; I will need to find a new job." "I can call Frank in the morning, maybe he will rehire me. " Danny replied, "You do not need to do that; I'll get a job." "Danny, there are not many jobs here, we can't live on McDonald's pay anymore." "I know," he said. "We may need to move!' "Frank, the mill is laying off people, Danny is one of them." He listened as I tried to be brave. "Can I be rehired?" "Mindy, we have filled your position, I am sorry," he replied. "I understand. Thanks, Frank." As I rose to leave his office, he added, "Mindy, hold on. Give me a few hours, and I'll call you." I didn't know what strings Frank pulled, but the new hire was let go, and she was hired at the credit union, all in one day. I got my job back. "What will we do with Ryan?" I asked Danny. "Maybe my grandmother can watch," he replied. Danny's grandmother, Oma, adored him. That assurance was enough for me to know Ryan would be in good hands. Great Oma became Ryan's caretaker while I was at work, as Danny headed south in search of work. "Kevin said I can stay with him and Lori, while I search for work," Danny said. Kevin and Lori were high school friends, living in Westbrook. It seemed like the only option for us at the time. "How long will you be gone?" I asked, my throat tight. "As long as it takes to find work." He continued talking, "We can't afford gas for me to drive back and forth...," but I was focused on "as long as it takes. Great Oma arrived like clockwork each day, thanking me for the opportunity to spend time with Ryan. I was still nervous about leaving him. Lunch breaks provided the perfect opportunity to check on them both. Nights were spent caring for Ryan and awaiting Danny's call. "Any luck today?" I'd ask. Danny replied, "Kind of. I got offered a job at a car wash place." "Danny, seriously, you don't need to do that." "Work is work," he replied. "I am giving it till the end of the week, if nothing else breaks, I am taking that job. "How are we doing with the listing of the trailer? "In truth, I was heartbroken to be selling our beautiful trailer. "Nothing, not even a call. I don't know what to do; no one is buying anything with the mill layoff. "A few days later Danny called with the news "Babe, I got a job. My military training in hydraulics has proven to be helpful! It pays about $7.25 per hour, nowhere near what I was making. But we can get by for now. Now we need a plan to get you and Ryan moved. "My head was spinning; we cannot live on $7.25 per hour...who will watch Ryan when we move...what will we do with the trailer? Yet I was proud of him. "That's great babe, it's a good start." Danny's Dad was a gentle man of few words. I don't recall him ever visiting me by himself, so when he was knocking at the door, I was taken back. I was further taken back by his aggressive approach. "Melinda, you need to fix this," he barked at me. "Fix it?" I choked back the tears, "How the hell do you expect me to do that?! We have no savings left, the trailer is not getting any offers, I am stuck in Millinocket and Danny is working in Westbrook." I traveled with Ryan to visit Danny on the weekend at his friend's home and then back again Sunday night to be ready for work on Monday morning. And he was telling ME to fix it! I was near tears, and he could sense it. "Can you move the trailer?" he gently asked. "I've already looked into it, there is a park in Brunswick, yet there are rules we can't afford," I replied. "What rules?" he asked. "We need to pay for a cement slab, and it needs to cover the oil tank area. It's at least $1,000 plus the cost of moving the trailer." I had $10.00 left in our savings! Junior is a good man; I knew his intentions were good. Yet, I was left feeling like I was failing. A few days later Junior was back at the door. "I will loan you the money. You'll need to pay it back," he said. "I appreciate the offer, yet I could never agree to it without speaking to Danny first." Danny said, "Babe, start packing, we are moving to Brunswick."

BRUNSWICK

"Bye Babe, I'll see you tonight, or tomorrow," Danny said as he kissed me and Ryan good-bye. Our plan to move to Brunswick was confusing to say the least. Portland was a reasonable commute to work; however, the job was short lived. "Babe, we will never pay the bills on the $7.25 an hour job. Maybe I can go to work." I would say. "I got this," Dan said. "We will figure it out." And we did. "Danny, you can't take a job in Rumford. That is a 2-hour drive, one way," I sighed. "It's a good job, it's what we need to do for now." Danny knew how to work in the paper mill. The Rumford mill was on strike, and he was being offered a good job, if he was willing to cross the picket line. There was judgment from those who worked with Danny at the mill in Millinocket.

"How can you cross the strike line?" some would ask him." Others just judged behind his back. I remember asking Danny, "Does what others say bother you?" He said, "What bothers me is not taking care of my family first. I wish there was another way, but this is the way." Danny was firm.

Danny worked 14-hour days, 2 hours travel to work, 2 hours travel home to Brunswick. When he said "Bye Babe, I see you tonight, or tomorrow" he wasn't kidding.

The days and nights rolled together. I was alone, except for Ryan. I did make a friend at the new mobile home park, and we would visit for hours over coffee. There was no spendable income, and I watched every penny. I filled my time as best I could. One of which was walking miles and miles each day with Ryan in the stroller. One day, I stopped at the park manager's office and explained my situation.

"Danny, I spoke with the park manager today, they sell trailers." I knew I had to do something, as I cleaned the hair out of the shower again. Danny doesn't stress, yet the stress of the long hours and the picket line was taking a toll on him. The hair loss was evidence of it.

"You love this trailer, are you sure you want to do that?" Danny asked. "I love you more, we will find another home one day," I said. Yet as I toured the town of Rumford, I was having second thoughts.

"Danny, I don't think Rumford is the place for us, do you?" It felt like Millinocket to me. Just driving through the town looking at rental property made my stomach hurt. Danny could sense my stress.

"I'm taking you to Auburn, you'll like it there" Danny said.

As I look back, I see myself so differently. At 24 years of age, I was transforming. The shy, quiet girl was leaving. In her place was a mom, a wife whose husband needed her to be strong.

"Babe, we got an offer on the trailer, it's not all we hoped for, yet it's a good offer. I will make a counteroffer of $2,000.00 more." I quickly followed that with "is that okay?" Danny's approval was still very much needed for me to find confidence. "Babe, I found a two-bedroom apartment in Auburn, we can do a 1-year lease to get us over the hurdle," again followed by "is this okay?" I could have signed a lease on a crack house, and he would have said "Good job." It didn't matter what I did or how I did it, he was proud of me. Any time off from work was rest time for Danny while I figured out our plans to move. Yet despite his exhaustion, he still made Ryan and me a priority. One night after dinner, Danny said, "How are you doing with all of this change?" "I decided to give up on my dream of being a Solid Gold Dancer" I replied. I was sure one day I would be a famous dancer. My time in California didn't open any doors. I figure now would be a good time to declare my end of the dream lol. Danny laughed and quickly jumped up. "You do not have an audition tape, that's the problem." We both laugh. He said, "Let's do one. Hurry, put on something cute and I'll set up the video recorder." With Pat Benatar on the turntable, my audition tape was made. "Now erase it!" I screamed. "No way, it's mine forever, you can be my Solid Gold Dancer!" To this day, Danny has my audition tape safely stored. "Ryan, I think we are packed!" I laugh as he crawls around the sealed boxes. This time I was sure to confirm our apartment was ready to move in. Saying good-bye to our trailer and Brunswick was easier than I thought it would be. I was eager to get on to the next chapter...the chapter in which I got to see my husband again! His hours were stabilizing at the mill and with an hour drive one way, it seemed like a light at the end of the tunnel. "Ryan, we got big news to share with Daddy tonight." He wasn't listening, he was pulling on the refrigerator door for ice cream! It would be one of our last meals at the trailer. I did my best to make the meal with unpacked dishes. Hours later, Ryan heard Daddy's car. He toddled to the door; it was a daily routine. "Ryan, what do you have in your ear?" Danny would say as he pulled out the treat of the day. It wasn't much. Maybe a piece of candy, or a small toy, but Ryan knew Daddy had magic powers! I was sure to inform Ryan, only Daddy had these powers! "Wow, you've been busy today" Danny said as he picked up Ryan and kissed me. With boxes everywhere, we sat down to enjoy our last family meal in my beloved trailer. "Babe, I may have made a mistake with the apartment." "What's wrong? Danny said calmly. He is always calm. "Maybe I should have gotten a 3 bedroom." It only takes him a second to know. We are having another baby! Our trailer was actually very comfortable, not double wide. Yet it had an addition for a small dining room and a larger living room. So, when Danny saw the apartment for the first time I was not surprised by his response. "Wow, this is small, are you sure?" It was small! A very small living room with a combined kitchen and an upstairs with one larger bedroom for us and a smaller one for Ryan. "It will be fine, there is a back yard for Ryan to play in and only one other tenant next door," I told Danny. "I'll need to share the laundry area, accessible to both units. But it's affordable and it's temporary." Little did I know the stairs across from Ryan's room would become my biggest challenge to date! "Why are you sleeping at the top of the stairs?" Danny asked as he tried to get me to go back to bed. "Your son thinks he is Houdini! He will not stay in his bed, and he is determined to climb over the gate," I cried. Really cried. At 4 months pregnant I was tired. "He is sleeping now," Danny said. "YUP, now he is, but it will not last, I am not taking the chance" I replied. Danny quietly picked up Ryan "Come to bed, he will sleep with us."

HOME

"What do you like best about this house?" I ask Dan, our bodies comfortably sprawled out on the newly carpeted living room floor, our gazes drifting upwards to the impressive 23-foot ceiling. It's a serene moment, just the two of us, waiting for the furniture that will soon make this house our home. As I've mentioned before, Danny is a thinker. He doesn't rush his responses; he lets his thoughts marinate. Sometimes, I wonder if he hears me at all, but then, like clockwork, he surprises me with a thoughtful answer. It's a quality of his that has taught me patience, well, sort of – you could say I'm a work in progress in that department. However, on this day, there's no lingering pause. "My favorite thing about our new house is how happy you are in it," Danny replies promptly. It's not just a casual comment; I can see the sincerity in his eyes. This house represents a significant milestone for both of us – a place we've never lived before. Sure, we've shared apartments and trailers, but owning a custom-built home was beyond my wildest dreams. Our time in that cramped 2-bedroom apartment in Auburn was a steppingstone, a sacrifice for the promise of something better in the future. We saved diligently, scrimping, and pinching pennies until we finally had enough for a down payment on this piece of land. I'd spend hours pouring over building inspiration books, but Danny always had a knack for spotting the unique and one-of-a-kind. Maybe that's why he's so fond of me; after all, I am one of a kind! He excitedly points out the advantages of our saltbox design, with the master bedroom and bath upstairs. "No more worries about kids climbing over gates to get downstairs," he laughs. "And with my shift work, I won't be encroaching on the kids' space, and vice versa." "I like that idea," I reply with a smile. And so, we decided that a saltbox home will be our next adventure. While I still rely on Danny for most major decisions, his approval provides me with a sense of confidence. However, I've also been growing as a problem solver, planner, and organizer, gradually shedding the skin of my younger self. Danny jokes at times, "Damn, I miss the girl I married; she always used to let me hold the remote control," with a chuckle. My mom's words echo in my head, "Lindy, life is about challenges; you'll forever be entering one, leaving one, or in the middle of one. That's just life. Don't worry about the challenges. Focus on the joy. "The responsibility of overseeing the home's construction mainly falls on my shoulders. While Danny works tirelessly to provide for our family, I take on the role of finding the right contractor, choosing fixtures, and sticking to our budget. "Mrs. Small, I've made a mistake. I underestimated the cost of building this home. I simply can't build it within the budget," confesses Paul, our contractor. My mom's advice rings in my ears, "It's just a challenge, Lindy. Find the solution. "I stand my ground. "Paul, we have a signed contract. I've only selected fixtures within the budget we agreed upon. I'm open to discussing why this isn't on budget, but I'm firm on our agreement." It feels surreal, but I'm holding my ground, facing the contractor head-on. "Mrs. Small, I simply miscalculated. I'll be losing money if I continue at this price," Paul admits. "So, what do you suggest we do now?" I ask. Paul instructs his team to pack up their tools until a new contract is in place. No more work until the issue is resolved. I wait for Danny to return from work; I don't often call him at work because I believe he's there to work, not to worry about family matters. However, today, as he opens the door, I'm bursting with stories. Danny is our rock, and his strength flows through me. "Maybe I can speak to the bank and request more money," I suggest. But Danny remains resolute. "No, he has an agreement with us. Lindy, if you need me to take tomorrow off, I'll do it." "No, let me handle this," I say. Paul demands more money, or the dream of our new home will vanish. On his days off, Danny rolls up his sleeves and begins working on the house, with me in tow. "Hold the sheetrock steady, Lindy!" "Danny, the ceiling is too high for me; I can barely reach it," I retort. Danny isn't always patient when we work on projects together, but somehow, we manage to get through them. "I hired a lawyer today," I inform

Dan. He scrutinized the contract and believes we have a strong case. In addition to the unfinished house, the contractor failed to pay the suppliers, resulting in a looming lien. "What's a lien?" I ask, feeling a sinking sensation in my stomach. Mom's words ringing in my ears..." always pay your bills Lindy and on time!" Going through the turmoil of a failed contract is something I wouldn't wish on anyone, but it's a learning experience. Since I was the project lead, I became the one to defend our case. Danny feels overwhelmed by the entire process. As we exit the courtroom, he turns to me, uncertainty in his eyes. "Did we win or lose?" The attorney reassures us, "You won, and your wife did an excellent job." "Tell me again what you like best about this house," Danny whispers, enveloping me in a warm hug as we gaze up at the magnificent 23-foot ceiling. "I love how happy you are in this house," he murmurs. I smile, grateful for our journey and the love that has carried us through every challenge.

LIFE HAPPENS FAST

Dan and I settled quickly into the rhythm of family life in our new home. Three kids came in rapid succession, keeping me on my toes. Ryan and Chelsey were off to school, and Ashley was peacefully napping in her crib, making it seem like just another ordinary day. "What time do you need to leave?" I asked Dan. He had the 3pm to 11pm shift at the mill. With the commute factored in, he knew he had to head out soon. Tucked in the nook of our living room was a home computer. In 1994, having a computer at home was still quite a novelty. Dan was engrossed in learning something new about it. Meanwhile, I was catching up on the latest Phil Donahue show and multitasking with the laundry while Ashley slept soundly, and the older kids were at school. "I can't believe you enjoy that show," Dan commented about the life-after-death conversation with Phil and his guest. "I believe in life after death," I replied, only to be interrupted by a growling noise, followed by Dan's arm stretched overhead. "Stop it," I thought he was teasing me. But then, suddenly, he was on the floor, his head colliding with the 6-foot window behind the office chair. I had no idea what was happening; all I knew was that it wasn't a joke. "911, what's your emergency?" I panicked and called for help. I tried to give our address, but the cord to the telephone didn't fit in the jack. With one arm cradling Dan and my foot holding the cord in place, I desperately tried to fix the connection. The call had disconnected. The line was dead! I did my best to quickly reinsert the cord into the jack and call back without moving my arm from his head. "911!" I didn't wait, "Please come quick, it's my husband. He's bleeding from his ear now." Dan had struck the window when he fell from the chair, and his head was bleeding profusely. It was a week before Christmas. As a stay-at-home mom, the responsibility weighed heavily on me to provide for a holiday and tend to Dan's health needs. Dan was the breadwinner, and now he was in the hospital for observation. We were all baffled. The doctor tried to reassure me, "Mrs. Small, these things are more common than we know. He may never have another seizure, or he may. We'll put him on medication. The good news is he'll be home for Christmas!" And he was. However, there was still much for me to do and leaving Dan at home, even for a moment, became too much for me. With no family nearby, we relied on each other and the kindness of neighbors. I'd sneak off to call a neighbor whenever I needed to run a quick errand. "Dick, would you mind watching the game with Dan while I run for groceries?" I'd ask, not one to easily trust. On one particular day, a quick trip to Kmart to pick up my kid's gifts on layaway and back was the plan.

However, when I arrived, I was met with unfortunate news: "I'm sorry, Dec 21 was the last day to pick up your layaway," the kind clerk explained. "Where are the gifts?" I inquired, my heart sinking. "We put them back on the shelves for others to purchase," she replied. "What happens to the money I prepaid?" She assured me she could refund it. As she counted out the $100.00, I could no longer hold back the lump in my throat. The stress of Dan's illness, the absence of gifts for the kids, and more weighed heavily on my mind. I apologized and explained that I couldn't make it to Kmart because my husband was in the hospital. Once again, I believe people come into our lives just when we need them most. On this day, it was the Kmart layaway clerk. She was an angel, saying, "Come on, honey, let's find your items." I wiped away the last of my tears and did my best to locate the special things the kids had hoped for. "That will do it," I said, giving the kind lady a heartfelt hug as I paid for the items. I remember this Christmas as one of my favorites. There weren't a lot of gifts under the tree, but I found creative ways to make it special, including scavenger hunts for the cherished items. Money would be tight without Dan's income. Yet, my husband was home. I understood the true meaning of a holiday blessing.

Melinda Small

GIFTS OF KINDNESS

"Do you hire women?" I asked our Prudential insurance agent as I prepared a cup of tea for both of us. I felt comfortable discussing anything in front of Dan, and he rarely reacted strongly. I had invited our life insurance agent to our home because I wanted to learn more about disability coverage. "Do we have any coverage for the time period in which Dan will be out of work?" I inquired. The agent explained the difference between life insurance and disability coverage. After absorbing the information, I realized that our current policy wouldn't provide a solution to our income challenges. I could hear the agent subtly encouraging Dan to consider a career change. "Dan, have you ever thought about becoming an insurance agent?" The words were barely out of the agent's mouth when I asked, "Excuse me, do you hire women as insurance agents?" That's how it all began. At the age of 35 I have very little work experience. I was making and selling dried flower crafts out of our basement as a means to help generate the extra income I desired to decorate our home. However, my real role was a stay-at-home mom and wife. I truly loved it. Caring for my children, my home, my husband filled me completely. "Dan, maybe I could get my insurance license," I suggested after our agent left. Dan assured me that I didn't need to work; he would find a way to provide for our family. But the mill where he worked was an hour away, he was on driving restrictions for six months, and he couldn't work around machinery, which was his primary job. " Honey, please don't worry about the money; I will figure it out," Dan reassured me as we lay in bed that night. It's strange how I remember the hours of conversation about everything and nothing during his recovery time. We'd tuck the kids in bed and then retreat to our own room. There were no TVs or cell phone distractions, just us. We were free to communicate openly, and I cherished every minute of it. I was quickly becoming the fixer of challenges. "I called the mortgage company today. I explained our situation, and they agreed to pause all payments for six months. However, the loan term has been extended by six months," I informed Dan. "Good job, babe," I could sense he was very proud of me for making that call. "I'll be back to work within six months," he said with determination. "Can we talk about the insurance thing again?" I asked. "I made some other calls today. It will cost about $100.00 for the study material and about $75.00 for the exam. I can make some dried flower arrangements and sell them to cover this cost." Once again, Dan assured me, "If it's something you want to do, I will support you, but don't do it because you think I can't provide. I promise I will

Dan assures me. "In fact, Dan's boss at the mill called that day and wanted to meet with us. "Us?" I exclaimed. "Do you think he'll fire you for getting sick and wants me there?" Dan chuckled at my reasoning. "No, I told him you would need to drive me," he laughed. "The boss said he would like to meet you." Dan's boss was friendly and seemed genuinely interested in Dan's health journey, our family, and our challenges. "Dan, you're a hard worker. Your team loves you," he said. "I've heard that you would be a good trainer and can write training manuals. The mill would like to offer you a desk job. We won't expect you to operate the machinery or be near them until your doctor says it's safe." He added, "If you accept this job, it comes with a wage increase." That's how Dan transitioned into a training position at the mill. Every morning at 5 am, I would wake the kids and drive Dan halfway to the mill in Rumford, with three sleepy kids in the back seat. Rain, sunshine, or snowstorm, we drove every morning he had work at 5 am. Dan would call from the mill to ensure we made it home safely. He would meet a co-worker who brought him the rest of the way. I would return home, put the kids back to bed for an hour before school. It didn't matter what the weather was; it was what we had to do. "Ugh, I'm so tired today," I told Dan. In truth, I was still stressed about leaving Dan at home alone. When he was at the Mill, he was around others that could help him if something happened. But being home alone with the kids was a different story. Ryan was a Boy Scout, and I had committed to a bottle drive. Dan said, "It will be good for you and Ryan to do it together," encouraging me to keep my commitment. So off we went to collect bottles from our neighbors. Hours later, the truck bed was filled with bottles, and Ryan told me where to drop them off. "May I ask how your husband is doing?" Nancy asked. It was the first time I had met her, and I was somewhat confused about how she knew about Dan. Nancy was a pleasant woman and a leader with organizing the bottle drive for the scouts, and I sensed her kindness quickly. Being a child of an alcoholic had trained me to always evaluate my surroundings. I explained Dan's blessings at the mill to her. She informed me that she was a private contractor with the mill and went there every day. She offered to pick up Dan, until he could drive himself. God had placed another angel in our path. To this day, I am thankful for her generosity. Never once did she express any burdens; she seemed genuinely happy to help. Dan enjoyed the conversations with Nancy during his drives to and from work. In truth, I've always had a difficult time accepting help; it makes me uncomfortable. Yet, I accepted her assistance with sincere gratitude for the blessing it brought to our lives.

LICENSED

With Dan back at work, I threw myself into the new venture of becoming an insurance agent. It wasn't a necessity, but I felt a deep sense of responsibility to contribute, to ensure that if anything were to happen again, we'd have a plan in place. As Ryan and Chelsey settled into school routines, Ashley began to enjoy the nearby daycare. She'd eagerly wave goodbye to me from the window, her excitement contrasting with the weight of guilt I carried about leaving her for a career. My initial plan had been to embrace full-time motherhood, and I loved every moment of it. But now, I was putting on a brave front, stepping into a new role. Over dinner one night, I mustered the courage to share, "I scheduled my exam. I think I'm ready." Exams always rattled me. Despite feeling fully prepared, the moment a test was in front of me, it was as if everything I knew vanished, replaced by nerves. Dan sensed my unease and kindly offered to drive me to Boston, the nearest testing site. I was grateful he was driving again; taking the test was challenging enough, the drive there would only make it worse. Looking back, I hadn't considered the long hours Dan would spend waiting in the car for me. As I walked back from the testing center 1.5 hours later, I struggled to hold back tears. "Stop it," Dan urged, unable to fathom the idea that I might have failed. "I'm not teasing. I did fail," I admitted, my voice catching. His unwavering belief in me made the bitter truth even harder to accept. "You didn't fail, you tried. And now you know more about the exam. You can take it again and pass next time," he reassured me. "Babe, that's all the money I saved for this! I have to pay every time I take the exam," I confessed, weighed down by guilt. I had used our hard-earned money for this pursuit, and I felt like I'd squandered it. Dan persisted in his encouragement for me to study and try again. I was hesitant, reluctant to spend the testing fee once more. But ultimately, I decided to take the chance. This time, my face beamed with joy as I proudly displayed my passing exam. It was September 1, 1995. "Toto, we're not in Kansas anymore!" I exclaimed, elated to officially be a licensed Life and Health agent in the state of Maine. With my newly acquired license, I stepped into this unfamiliar world of insurance. Each day brought its own set of challenges, a stark contrast to the comfort and routine of motherhood. There were moments when doubt crept in, questioning if I was capable of mastering this new role. As I delved into my career, I grappled with the internal conflict of leaving my cherished role as a stay-at-home mom. The echoes of Ashley's waves and the ache in my heart lingered. Ryan and Chelsey would arrive home after school to a new routine. No mom to greet them, to love on them with baked goods after a day at school. Balancing the demands of this new career with my yearning for the familiar rhythms of motherhood became an emotional tightrope walk of guilt. Dan, always my rock, stood by me through it all. He was the steady hand that held me up when my resolve wavered. His belief in me was unwavering, a lifeline I clung to in moments of self-doubt. "You're stronger than you think, Lindy," he would remind me, his words a balm to my anxious soul. The days turned into weeks, and weeks into months. Slowly, I found my footing in the insurance world. The knots of apprehension began to loosen, replaced by a growing sense of confidence. I started to see glimmers of the person I was becoming, the professional woman emerging from the cocoon of motherhood. Yet, there were still days when the yearning for the simplicity of my old life would wash over me. Ryan and Chelsey had added pressure to their routine as well. I needed help at home, start the laundry, watch your little sister, begin dinner.... The pull of motherhood was a constant, a powerful force that tugged at my heartstrings. I missed the uninterrupted hours with my children, the unhurried moments of play and discovery. But with every successful policy I sold, every client I helped navigate the complexities of insurance, a new sense of purpose blossomed within me. The lines between motherhood and career began to blur, and I realized that this transformation wasn't a betrayal of my old self, but a natural evolution. I earned trips, cruises, awards, bonus money. To offer my family the benefits of these perks seemed to help balance the guilt. As the years passed, I grew into my role as an insurance agent eventually becoming the president of my own agency, Pinetree Retirement Planning. The emotional struggle that once weighed heavily on me gradually transformed into a quiet sense of fulfillment. I learned that it was possible to hold onto the essence of who I was as a mother while embracing the challenges and triumphs of my career. Looking back, I can now see that this journey was a testament to the strength of a woman's spirit, a mom's spirit, a wife's spirit. It taught me that transformation isn't about leaving behind the past, but about carrying it forward with grace and resilience. And in that delicate dance between motherhood and career, I discovered the depths of my own capabilities and the boundless love that fueled it all.

GOODBYE MOM

Everything happened so swiftly. Just before mom's procedure to induce a self-imposed coma, Mom's voice on the phone reassured me not to rush. "Lindy don't come now. I'll need you when they wake me up." She had been ailing for months, yet the cause remained elusive. Bad health never seems to choose a convenient time, and this week was exceptionally challenging. Chelsey was graduating 8th grade, and I was overseeing the move of my growing insurance office to a spacious 3500 sq foot building. The logistics of the move should have been straightforward, but my thoughts were consumed by Mom. "How is she doing?" Dan inquires as I hang up the phone. "I have a terrible feeling," is all I manage to say. Those intrusive worries were back, nudging me along. But there was furniture to move, equipment to organize. It seemed to be everywhere, and I was the only one who knew where each piece belonged in our new office. "Honey, I've got this. You need to go," Dan insists. "What about Chelsey's graduation, what about..." He stops me mid-sentence. "You know where you need to be. Go. I've got this." "Okay thank you... I'm taking Ashley with me," I reply, hurrying out of the parking lot to pick up Ashley. Maybe I needed her with me. Maybe I wanted to relieve some pressure from Dan and the kids to care for her at age 5. Either way, she was easy to bring along. "Mom will be back in a few days. I need to see Nana, she isn't feeling well." Without a word, the kids help Ashley pack a few things, aware of her young age. Ryan and Chelsey will stay home with Dan. I didn't want Chelsey to miss her graduation, but I also didn't want to miss it. When I arrive in Millinocket, Mom is already in her self-induced coma. "May I sit with her?" I asked the nursing staff. And I did. For days, I waited, hoping for signs of improvement, for her to wake up. There were signs, but I couldn't see them. "Mom's mouth is drooping today," I tell the doctor. "Mom's temperature seems high today," I report. I can still feel the heat from her body. I knew she needed to cool down. "May I have some cool bathwater and a cloth?" I ask the nurse. Alone in the room, just me and Mom. I gently remove the sheets and her nightgown and begin to carefully wipe her down with the cool cloth. Each stroke of the cloth feels like a message from her body, a silent narrative of the life she lived. I couldn't help but reflect on the strength she embodied, having undergone a double mastectomy years prior. " Oh Mom. What a life you've lived," I whisper, continuing the process of cooling her down. "Thank you, Mom, for everything." And then, Dee Dee arrives. I think she knew Mom was nearing the end, but it's her words that finally pulled me out of denial. "Lindy, you're going to have to tell her it's okay to go. I knew she was right and simply nodded and hugged her. "The doctor addresses us, his voice a solemn reflection of the gravity of the situation. "Mrs. Small, your mom's fever has reached 110 degrees. Brain damage has occurred, her mouth is drooping. We can't identify the root cause. Despite our efforts, only a UTI is evident. Your mom is alive because of life support. I'll give you time to decide what you wish to do next. "For years, it was just me and Mom, thick and thin. And now, here we were. Just me and Mom. "Oh, Momma," I cry softly as I nestle in beside her. "It's time for you to go. I'll miss you, but I'll be okay. You did well, Momma. "I make the calls to my brothers, Sam, and Scott. I call Dan. I politely ask if they have any opinions on what they want done, but in the end, I know this is my decision to make for Momma. "Mom, it's time to go. Your wings await you," I tell her as I crawl into bed beside her. Dan and the kids arrive later the same day. We all gather around her bed, sharing stories and love. Out of the mouth of babes comes Ashley. "Mom, did you see that?" she exclaims. "The angels just took Nana, and in this moment, her heart stopped, and the monitor went flat."

Melinda Small

OCT 15TH 2010

"Babe, I need to talk with you," Dan's face bears a serious expression. My heart skips a beat as he speaks. "Something odd happened today. I had blocks of time where I felt I was lost, drifting away." My attempt to stay calm is challenged. My insides are trembling as I recall the first seizure so many years ago. However, I dismiss the thoughts and turn to learning more.. "What do you mean?" I inquire. "I'm not sure. I'm just telling you, so you'll know," Dan replies, his voice filled with uncertainty. I'm keenly aware of the gravity of his words. "How do you feel now?" I press, concern etching my features. "Okay, just odd," he murmurs, his eyes reflecting a mix of confusion and apprehension. "Maybe you need some rest. Let's go to bed," I suggest. It's already 10pm on October 15, 2010. I rub his back as we lay together, exchanging quiet conversations. Soon, Dan drifts off into sleep, but I remain vigilant, one eye open. Around 3am, I wake up. There's no pressing need, but perhaps a distraction would help. I mutter a soft prayer of gratitude for the peaceful night and return to bed. "Babe, are you okay?" I call out gently, sensing something's amiss. "Babe? Babe?" My heart races as I hear the sound of toothpicks breaking in the darkness. I know instinctively that this night won't end peacefully. It's a skill I've honed, a result of past experiences. I recently described to the doctor, "It was like watching the incredible hulk, he just kept growing in muscle. His body was like a rock." Dan is in the midst of a grand mal seizure. Panic surges through me as I rush to Ashley's room. "Ashley, listen carefully. Drive to the end of the driveway in your car and keep flashing your lights. The ambulance can't miss our driveway." It's a lot for a half-asleep Ashley to process, but she manages, driven by the urgency of the situation. Returning to the bedroom, I find Dan on his knees, rocking back and forth, his moans a desperate plea for help. "Help me, help me," he repeats, a mantra of distress. I push down my own fear and tears. Not now. Not yet. "It's okay, honey. I'm here. You're okay. I'm here," I repeat, my voice a steady anchor. "You're safe. Come back to me." I continue these soothing words until the seizure finally subsides. It's unlike any previous episode. I know to remain calm, gently rubbing his arms and legs, desperate for him to feel my touch. Fifteen minutes later, he begins to return. "I need to get in bed," he mumbles, too weak to stand. I help him up, though I'd rather he stayed on the floor. "Mom, the paramedics are here," Ashley informs me. Zack and Zoey our loyal labs, sensing the urgency, stay close, protective. I hurried to secure them in our bathroom while the paramedics assess Dan. He's still disoriented, defensive, convinced someone has intruded our home. My voice seems to be the only thing that soothes him. I do my best to assure him that we're all safe. "Ashley, you need to call Ryan and Chelsey. Tell them to meet us at the hospital," I direct, though Ashley looks near fainting. I need to return to Dan. She needs me, but I can't help her right now are more thoughts of guilt that race through my mind. The rest is a blur. I'm not sure if the ambulance beats us to the hospital or if our children do. But Dan is rushed in for observation. "Mrs. Small, tell us how he fell," the nurse asks. "Fell? He didn't fall. He rolled out of bed gently, but no fall," I responded, confused. Why are they asking me this? The nurse presses further, probing for details. "I'm sure there was no fall. Why are you asking me this?" I insist, a hint of impatience in my voice. "There are signs of internal bleeding. We need to know why," the nurse explains. Dan continues to reassure me, "Babe, it's okay. I'm just sore now." Ryan advises me to leave the room. "Why do I need to leave?" I question, but Ryan insists, "You don't need to see this. They're going to give Dad a needle to help with the pain. I'll stay with him. Go sit down with Ashley and Chelsey." Ashley, in her senior year, calls upon Timmy, her boyfriend for support. Chelsey and her husband, Fred, have arrived, along with Ryan's bride of just a few days, Christina. They all reassure me that Dad will be fine; they just need to know the cause of the bleeding. "Mrs. Small, your husband will need immediate surgery. Both of his rotator cuffs are out of place, in his back," the nurse informs me. I'm dumbfounded, struggling to comprehend the severity of the situation. Dan reassures me, "Babe, come here." I reach out, careful not to hurt him further. "Give me a kiss. Don't worry, I'll come back", and he is gone to surgery in a flash. "The surgery will take longer," the nurse adds. I hear a buzzing in my ears, but I shake it off, forcing myself to focus. "The left shoulder took hours to reset, but the right one is more complicated. There's no blood flow, and they'll have to build a new rotator cuff." I sign the consent form quickly, and in a flash, the surgeon is gone again. October 15th is also my daughter-in-law's birthday. Newly married, she's still finding her place within our family, holding herself slightly apart. We had planned an afternoon dinner for her, and I still want to go through with it. I want her to know that through thick and thin, we're family. "Mom, you need to eat," Chelsey reminds me. "Yes, let's have a pizza party with cake!" I suggest, determined to keep our promise to Christina. All the kids are in motion, organizing the impromptu celebration. "Mom, you take a nap in Dad's room. We'll be back with pizza and cake!" Christina objects, but we are all resolute as she looks to Ryan for support. He shrugs and says, "it's what we do." Gathered together, we anxiously await Dan's return from shoulder replacement surgery. I wish I could say the story ends here, with just one surgery and a return to normalcy. However, in the days following his recovery, Dan's strength wanes, and even walking becomes a challenge. Frustrated, I persistently voice my concerns: "My husband is resilient. If he's not progressing as expected something else must be amiss. I demand an MRI of his back." Despite facing resistance, I refuse to be silenced. "Listen," I interject firmly, "there will be an MRI today."

I wish I had been mistaken. The MRI confirmed my fears: Dan's injuries extended beyond his shoulders alone. His lower spine was fractured, with vertebrae shifting from the broken ones at the base of his spine. As the days pass, Dan continues to make strides in his recovery. Each step forward is a victory, no matter how small, and together we confront moments of frustration and pain. "Babe, are you awake?" Dan's voice breaks through the silence of the hospital room. I'm always awake, always ready to attend to his needs. "Yes, I'm here," I respond from the makeshift sleeping chair beside his bed.

"I want to sing a song to you," Dan announces unexpectedly. I chuckle softly. Dan isn't known for his singing prowess. Yet, on this night, he serenades me. Whether it's the medication or his overwhelming love, I couldn't care less. We both dissolve into laughter, cherishing the heartfelt melody expressing his love for me. My strong husband embarked on a journey of recovery, a path that would be difficult for both of us, and for our kids. "What are you doing?" I ask, spotting Dan sitting in the dimly lit room. "I thought I'd host a pity party today, just for one. It'll be a short one, because I've got life to live after," he quips. Complications from medication lead to esophagus issues and more hospital stays. His strength to overcome never ceases to amaze me. He's had to learn to say, "I can't do that," a challenging transition for the man of the family. In this, we've had our battles. "Let me carry that," I'll insist. His quiet frustration is palpable. I've learned about boundaries—well, I'm learning about boundaries and so is he. If he needs to carry something heavy, I step back. He knows he'll pay the price later, but at that moment, he needs to do it. I've learned to look away when it's too much for me to watch, putting faith in him and in God. I often tell him, "I wish I could go back to the moment you told me something odd was happening." His response is always, "And what do you think you could have done differently to change the outcome?" I have a full list of what I could have done differently, but in reality... nothing would have changed. With Dan's determination and a support system that always rallies around us, we've navigated this unexpected journey. Chelsey, now married to Fred, and Ryan, recently wed to Christina, have become pillars of strength. Their love and commitment to our family is both reassuring and uplifting. Meanwhile, Ashley, in her senior year, faced her own set of challenges. She made the difficult decision to move out of our home, seeking a sense of independence. Her world had been shaken, and her once unwavering sense of security was now tinged with uncertainty.

The transition was undoubtedly tough on her and tough on me to watch. As the days pass, Dan continues to make strides in his recovery. Each step forward is a victory, no matter how small. There are moments of frustration and pain, but we face them head-on, together. Our bond has only deepened through this experience, and our love for each other shines brighter than ever. Through it all, I've learned the true power of family, of unity in the face of adversity. We've come to understand that life's unexpected twists are opportunities for growth, for discovering the strength we never knew we had. And so, as we forge ahead, I hold on to the belief that we can overcome anything that comes our way. With faith, love, and unwavering support, we'll continue this journey, one step at a time. The years that followed brought about significant changes in our family dynamic.

Melinda Small

MY PRIDE AND JOY

Dan's discomfort was palpable, etching lines of worry on his face. It was clear that something was deeply troubling Chelsey. The joy of becoming a grandmother not too long ago was still fresh, yet an unspoken sense of unease lingered beneath the surface, intensifying my maternal instincts. When Chelsey dropped off Brody, Dan gently suggested I talk to her. "Honey, Chelsey will open up when she's ready. She's always needed her own time to process things. Pushing won't help," I responded to Dan's request, understanding Chelsey's need for space. Still, I decided to give it a shot. As I approached Chelsey, her guarded posture told its own story. She was clearly navigating uncertain territory. "Honey, talk to me. What's going on?" I urged. Her words still echo in my ears, "Mom, you could never understand!" Little did she know. Chelsey's demeanor spoke volumes about her troubled marriage. She didn't need to explicitly tell me; the signs were all there. Cooking is Chelsey's way of expressing love. She could dedicate an entire day to crafting a beautiful meal, only for Fred to opt for a frozen $1 pizza instead. Often, she found herself alone while Fred spent hours playing pool. The divide was painfully evident. Fred and Chelsey had been friends since 6th grade, and they became homeowners and newlyweds at the tender age of 19. By 23, they had a baby, and sadly, their marriage was coming to an end. Tigger held a special place in Chelsey's heart, having been her first love. It was always Chelsey and Tigger, a gift from her dad and me in her 7th-grade year. Tigger, a fiercely protective Shih Tzu, shared a unique bond with Chelsey that only they understood. My heart broke when I learned of her, alone at home after only hours of holding her Tigger as the vet ended her last breath. Fred was off to play pool. I gently knocked on her door. "Honey, can I come in?" She had a unique way of handling stress, holding it tight, letting very few people inside. However, she did open the door for me, and we talked "Mom, I just want to go to bed" Chelsey wasn't just my daughter anymore, she was a mom. A strong woman was unfolding. So, on this night that she spat at me "MOM, you could never understand" I understood all too well. Chelsey was unhappy and her marriage was ending. There are many emotions experienced in the ending of a relationship. However, pride was at the top of my list. "Mom, it's just stuff, I can get more stuff later." she said while sitting on the floor holding Brody as Fred and his parents loaded truck after truck of the furniture and personal belongings once shared by them. "I have all I need in my arms; she says as she holds Brody tightly. Let them take the couch, the food in the cupboards, take everything... Soon Chelsey was working at Legends as a bartender, and I watched Brody as she mustered the courage to learn how to support them. From stay-at-home mom to sole provider. Yup, it was pride I was feeling as I watched her rebuild her life. My dad often referred to me as his pride and joy. Chelsey is my pride and joy. "Chelsey, when are you going on a date with him?" Neither of us had to say his name. Robbie was always a step away. It didn't matter that Chelsey had rejected him in the past. When a man loves a woman, he loves her completely. Dan and I were in the middle of opening a new restaurant and Robbie found himself there, ready to lend a helping hand as he repaired this and built that for our new company. Robbie is a man. By every definition that Dan and I describe as a man. What a man means to a home, to a wife, to a family, to his children. Dan and I didn't make it easy on Robbie from day 1. After all, Chelsey is our beautiful bright spirited child. When Robbie asked for her hand in marriage, we were clear. "Chelsey is a grown woman, and she is a package deal with Brody. We trust Chelsey, if she says yes, then our blessing follows." Robbie is not a stepdad; he is just dad to both Brody and Ellie. I see the way he looks at Chelsey. It's the way Dan looks at me. Full of unconditional, unwavering love. We are blessed to call Robbie our son! In all honesty, I am sure I've come up a bit short for Chelsey at times, communication can be challenging. However, there is a deep and profound connection that my heart feels. There is no limit to how I would support Chelsey in any challenge. In her path towards independence and finding love again, my role as her mom changed. Much like my own role with my own mom changed as I found my own independence. In this, Chelsey and I are alike. I often ask myself if my mom knew how much I loved her. If I said thank you enough for the crucial role she played in my life, by providing guidance and a safe space for me to grow, even while I expressed, I no longer needed her. I pray Chelsey never questions this and simply knows she is my pride and joy. I am blessed to call her my middle child, my laughter, the amazing mom to my grandchildren.

MOM, I LOVE YOU

"Hurry up, you'll be late," I called out to Ashley, knowing she had her own sense of time. Eighth grade was a pivotal year for her, and I was determined not to miss a single moment. Our daily car rides to school became cherished opportunities to catch up with her. But today was different. "Mom, it will be fine, we have time," Ashley assured me as she gathered her school supplies. The usual banter filled the five-minute ride from home to school, but as I approached the parking lot, my heart sank. There were so many cars. "Ashley, why are there so many cars here?" I asked, a sinking feeling in my chest. Then it hit me—it must be Pastry with Parents Day. Ashley was oblivious to my emotions as tears welled up in my eyes. "Oh, yeah. I think it's that," she said casually. To her, my response seemed like anger. "MOM, I didn't know you liked pastries so much! I'm sure we can still go in and get one," Ashley offered, trying to calm me. But the event was ending, and I had missed my last Pastry with Parents. My heart ached, but I reassured Ashley, "It's fine, sweetheart," as I wiped away the tears. When I returned home, Dan sensed immediately that something was wrong. "I missed Pastry with Parents," I confessed, curling up on his lap and crying like a child. "Oh no," he murmured, rocking me gently. "It will be okay." However, there was little time to mourn my loss. "I have a staff meeting, I need to go," I told Dan, forcing myself to pull away. The staff meeting followed its usual agenda, but I couldn't shake my distraction. My team could sense it too. Lisa excused herself and returned with a large tray of pastries. "Dan called," she said, a warm smile on her face, "we have pastries to enjoy with you!" I couldn't help but burst into tears. "I know this is silly, but it was my last one," I sobbed, a mixture of relief and gratitude washing over me. Throughout the day, I received texts from Ashley, expressing her apologies. "I really am sorry, Mom," she wrote. "It's okay, honey. I overreacted. I'll pick you up after school," I reassured her. When I pulled up to the school later, Ashley bounced out of the doors and into the car. "I got two!" she exclaimed, unwrapping the napkin with joy. Ashley is my baby, my last opportunity to be a young mom. There was a special place in my heart for her that nothing else could fill. Maybe it's that way for many moms as the last grows away from them. As she approached her thirties, she reached out to me with an invitation to visit the botanical gardens for their evening lights display. "Yes, Ashley, I would love to do this with you," I replied. Ashley is a remarkable soul, radiating beauty from the inside out. Her heart is my heart, and she often puts others before herself, fearing she might hurt them. She found a way to turn what could have been my worst Pastry with Parents Day into the best one. Yet, I also had to find a way to let her go. One of the hardest things I've even done in life. Six minutes after receiving her text, my intuition kicked in. Moms just know. Despite the late hour and no alert tone, I picked up my phone. "Are you awake by chance?" she ask. "Yes, what's up?" I try to remain calm at 3am. Ashley's voice trembled. She was in pain, unable to sleep, and desperately needed reassurance. My first priority was to calm her. Ashley was living alone for the first time in 8 years. "What did you eat?" I inquired. "A few bites of a Subway salad," she responded. "Do you want to go to the emergency room?" As we talked, I could hear her retching in the background. "Do you want me to come to your place?" I asked, ready to be there in a heartbeat. But Ashley declined, and I assured her it might just be a bad reaction to the tuna or a virus from the recent grad party for Brody. "I feel sweaty," she confessed, her anxiety evident. "Get two towels and cool them with water. Use one now and put the other in the fridge for later if you still feel sweaty," I advised, hoping to provide some comfort. "Mom, I'm already so thin, I can't lose more weight," Ashley choked back the tears. I reminded her of the progress over the past few years and how proud I was of her. In this moment, I recall my mom standing from dad at the AA meeting. "Proud", she had said! I now understood the reasoning. I was equally proud of Ashley and her own journey! "Mom, I love you," she said, a sentiment that meant the world to me. "I love you too, Ashley," I replied. "Okay, I'm going to try to sleep for a bit now," she said. "Call me anytime if you need me." "I will," she promised. Those three words, "I love you," held immeasurable meaning for me. It had been eight years since I last heard them, eight years of letting her find her own way, 8 years of drug addiction, 8 years of absence as she refused to reach out for help or support, sharing her secret with only her sister. However, tonight I was her first call in her hour of need. In this moment, I knew Ashley would be well and healthy once again.

FAMILY

Ryan, my firstborn, is a beacon of stability and kindness, a paragon of unwavering ethics. The saying goes, "A daughter is a daughter all of her life, a son is a son till he takes his wife." Yet, in witnessing the partnership of love and support that Christina and Ryan embody for our family, I've come to understand that this adage couldn't be further from the truth. This truth was never more evident than on the Mother's Day when Ryan spent the entire day with me on a food tour, wholeheartedly supported by Christina. I'll admit, I initially felt a bit awkward having Ryan all to myself on such a special day, but I also felt incredibly loved and honored to share that intimate moment with him. Years have passed since that day. Ryan and Christina are now the proud parents of two beautiful daughters. Ryan juggles running a private business with a successful full-time career, firmly establishing himself as the provider. Meanwhile, Christina stands as the unwavering support, enabling all that Ryan achieves. I vividly recall the day I first met her. It was a warm summer's day, and Ryan invited her to our lake house. Dan and I were invited to meet her. In mere moments, I knew that Christina would one day be his bride. "Mom, I plan to go to camp on Sunday and take the boat out with the family for a ride," Ryan informed me. I explained that I couldn't make it on Sunday due to one of Dan's tournaments. An hour later, he called back, "Okay, we've shifted the plans to Saturday. Join us if you can." A swift call to Chelsey, and she responded, "Yup, Brody and Evelyn are already excited about it. We'll head up too." Another call to Ashley, and she exclaimed, "I'll get ready. Pick me up!" Just like that, another family day was set in motion. Dan was still in recovery from surgery, and a boat trip wasn't in his cards. We decided to stay on land and waved goodbye to our family as they set off for their adventure without mom and dad, a new experience for us. My thoughts drift to a future when it will be them alone, a time when mom and dad may not always be around. My heart swells with love as I reflect on how it all began—Ryan, Chelsey, and Ashley transformed into Ryan, Christina, Evelyn, Katherine, Chelsey, Robbie, Brody, Ellie, and Ashley, with a pack of dogs to keep them company.

TRUSTING

Over the past two years, I've embarked on a profound journey of self-discovery. This odyssey was partly guided by the process of writing this book, and partly shaped by the trials and tribulations life threw my way. It all began in Vegas, where Dan and I first heard the term "Covid." We briefly considered extending our stay, thinking the virus would pass, only to find out that the hotel was closing its doors. Looking back, I often wonder why I supported the opening of Legends so soon after Dan's grand mal seizure in 2015. Perhaps it was to help him start a new chapter in his life. But life has a way of steering us, and I followed along. Then came March 15, 2020, when states started implementing shutdowns to curb the spread of COVID-19. Just months prior, we had invested in a $700,000 building to expand the restaurant. The timing felt surreal. As I packed perishable goods, I couldn't help but think of our employees and how they would cope without income. And what about Dan and me, and the building we'd just acquired? I reminded myself, "First things first, Lindy. Stay strong and trust. Trust doesn't come easy for me. I'm more of a fixer, finding solace in that role. But this situation was beyond my control. As the walk-in cooler emptied and the doors were locked, I went home. "How did it go?" Dan asked. I choked back tears, "It was okay. The perishables are gone; the frozen items are in the freezers as best as I could manage." Andy, my kitchen manager, had thought ahead, leaving the kitchen in impeccable shape for the uncertain days ahead. But I felt a need to be there. As Dan embraced me, he reassured me, "It'll be alright, don't worry." My daily routine, once so steadfast, crumbled by day four of the lockdown. Four days in the same pajamas, no shower, no makeup. Just me, glued to the TV. "We need to get out of this house," Dan declared. "Is it safe?" We were uncertain of what was permitted or frowned upon. "We won't leave the car; it'll be fine," Dan assured. Trusting him, I showered, changed into fresh clothes, and off we went. The streets were deserted, businesses shuttered. We drove in silence. "I've been researching how businesses can qualify for help," I told Dan a few days later. "I've also reached out to the CDC. We can serve guests in their cars, but not in the building." "Like an old-fashioned car hop?" Dan mused. "Exactly! I'm contacting employees to see who can assist. I'll also set up takeout ordering," I rambled on. And so, it began. We launched an online ordering website. Our parking lot was transformed into a car hop for food service. "We can open a patio if I can find the furniture and the funds to buy it," I informed Dan. He drove me to different towns, scouring Lowe's for chairs and tables. " Ugh, honey, that was another $4,000," I sighed as I made the final purchases. Piece by piece, we assembled enough matching furniture for a 50-seat patio. Doubts nagged at me. Would this investment pay off, or would it deepen our debt? Dan sensed my worry. "Don't worry," he reassured. I have some fears in life, and money is one of them. Mom's words echo in my ears, "Pay your bills, Lindy, and pay them on time." I remember the day when she asked the bank manager if she could keep the dining room table during their bankruptcy filing. The answer was a heart-wrenching no. Some memories never fade. The fear of financial instability is palpable at times. I tread cautiously when it comes to managing money. And here I was in 2020, with a new commercial building, two businesses, and a government shutdown! " What's wrong?" Dan inquired. I was on the verge of tears. "I just want some normalcy! I want to go to my favorite restaurant and have table service." The weight of it all felt overwhelming that day. "Get in the car," Dan commanded. His patience was wearing thin, with everything, including my mood. Soon enough, he was in an apron, lobsters in the pot, playing the role of a waiter. With a towel draped over his arm and a bottle of wine… "Today's wine is a white something," he ventured. I laughed. He had no clue about wines. Together, we savored table service at my cherished restaurant. We shared laughter and tears, surrounded by the 8,000 square feet of space that would become Legends' new home, with just the two of us. It's been a journey. We kept our doors open. In fact, we added 35 more parking spaces in the midst of Covid. We installed a patio door and revamped the entrance at Legends. Our sales doubled from our previous peak year. With each investment, I'd ask, "Can we afford this?" and Dan's response was always, "Don't worry." But I still worried. In all honesty, the past years caught up with me recently. The burden became too much. "You need to stop trying to fix everything," Dan advised. His words left me puzzled. We often misunderstand each other. He's from Mars, and I'm from Venus. "I don't understand," I retorted. He walked away, exasperated. "What happens if I don't fix the employee who's consistently late?" I pondered aloud. "Dan, come back. I need you to explain." He was visibly irritated, but he tried once more. "I've been telling you for years, Lindy, you try to fix everything. Some things you can't. If an employee is unreliable, you need to find a replacement." "But what if I can't find new employees?" I started to say, but he cut me off. "You can do anything, you just need to change your thinking, honey." It took me ten days to hire all the employees we needed to fill our open spots. Former (amazing) employees reached out, eager to return to Legends. This story isn't just about Covid, Legends, or employees. It's about me stepping into a new chapter of trust, of letting go of the need to fix, and learning to accept. It won't be easy. For over 60 years, I've honed the art of fixing or attempting to prevent bad things from happening. But bad things do happen. And so do good things. That's life.

Melinda Small

I HEARD HIM COMING

April 13th, "No," was my immediate response when Dan suggested bringing a white lab into our home. It had been almost a year since we bid farewell to Zack and Zoey, our beloved pair of yellow labs. The pain of their departure was still raw, and I had adamantly sworn that I would never open my heart to another dog. However, resisting Dan's persistence was proving to be a challenge for me. Gradually, my resolve began to weaken as he shared videos of irresistibly cute white labs frolicking about. "But how would we even go about getting Oliver?" I finally relented, curiosity tugging at my heart. "Perhaps we could embark on a road trip," Dan suggested tentatively. The idea was taking shape in my mind. "We could take a month off and journey to Arkansas. And so, the story began, Oliver was our adorable white lab!

April 13th, a day forever etched in my memory, a turning point that marked a profound shift within me. Some may attribute it to being an empath, while others might say that growing up with an alcoholic father sharpened my sensitivity to the emotions around me.

Regardless, this heightened awareness keeps me on edge, attuned to the world. On this particular day, Dan and I found ourselves in Pennsylvania, a brief weekend getaway centered around a visit to the Billiards Expo. Usually, our faithful companion, Oliver, would stay with his trusted pet care provider if we traveled. But this time, all options were booked. "We can take him with us," I suggested to Dan, foreseeing that Oliver would make for an excellent walking companion. Events unfolded swiftly. We'd been at the hotel for about half an hour, and Dan was eager to check in on his friends at the expo. "Go ahead, I'll be fine," I assured him. The evening was growing late, yet it was a beautifully warm night—the first after a long, harsh winter. "Come on, Oliver, let's squeeze in one more walk." I leash my eager puppy. The hotel grounds were lovely, well-lit, with inviting walking paths. Still, my empathic senses were on high alert. "Why am I feeling so anxious? Calm down," I told myself. Despite my internal reassurances, I made the decision to turn back after just a hundred feet along the building's side. What was causing this charge of apprehension when there wasn't a soul in sight? I couldn't put my finger on it. Then, I heard it—didn't see it, just heard it—and I knew! A woman's scream pierced the air from about two hundred feet away, and in that moment, I knew her dog was headed our way. "Pick him up and run," my inner voice commanded. But Oliver, at nearly 70 pounds, was not an easy lift. I struggled to get his front legs over my shoulders, but he was wrenched away from me. A pit bull had clamped onto Oliver's lower body. "Protect his neck," my inner voice insisted. I positioned myself between Oliver's upper and lower body, engaging in my own battle. Punches had no effect on the pit bull. I lay on my back, kicking with both feet at the dog's face. Still, there was no response as the grip tightened. I removed my sandal and used it as a weapon. Still, nothing. "Pray," the voice urged. "Pray." I sank to the ground, hands raised, eyes and head tilted skyward, fingers reaching out. "Sweet Jesus, please help me. Please, sweet Jesus, I need you." I repeated the plea, my eyes on the heavens. And then, a profound peace washed over me. I felt my mother with me. Silence enveloped us. Oliver was on the run. I saw my beloved pup pause and glance back at me. "No, Oliver, run!" He obeyed, but the pit bull was hot on his heels, and so was I. "Retrieve your sandal, it's your weapon," my inner voice reminded me. I retrieved the first one I found and raced to find Oliver. The pit bull had caught up with him, launching a second assault. Screams filled the air, and I added my own, louder and longer. "HELP ME!" I was now at the front of the hotel, nearer to the entrance. There were people, but so few were willing to help. Then, I spotted them. Two, maybe three men. One held the pit bull, Oliver hanging from the dog's lockjaw. "Who has a knife?" I shouted. Within seconds, the blade materialized. I looked at the dog's owner, my voice now softer, pleading. "Please, you need to stop this. Your dog is killing him. Give them permission to stop it." She nodded. The man asked, "Is that a yes?" I said, "Yes", she said "yes." Every second was crucial. I looked at her again, asking for confirmation. She repeated, "Yes." In an instant, the pit bull's throat was slit. Blood cascaded like a waterfall, soaking Oliver's once-snow-white fur. My vision swayed, everything moving in slow motion. I didn't witness Oliver's escape; I just knew he was gone once more. I scrambled to my shoeless feet and sprinted across the asphalt. "Lord, please, do not let him get hit by a car." But I couldn't find him. "He ran into the building," a voice called out. The automatic entry doors were the perfect escape route for Oliver. I ran in a frenzy, calling out, "Oliver, Oliver, Oliver." "Ma'am, you're bleeding. You need to wrap your hand. Your dog is down the hall," the stranger urged me. "207, 577, 7xxx," I repeated what felt like a hundred times. "Dan Small, please call him." I could hear people speculating. I needed my husband! "Her husband must be in room 207", I heard someone say. "Call 207, 577, 7xxx," I persisted, needing to ensure I had a contact in case I passed out. In life, there are moments that alter us, that shape us into something different. This was my moment.

UNCONDITIONAL

The attack on Oliver marked a turning point, a shift in my being. It's as if the very core of who I am underwent a transformation.

Six decades plus of life, I am a tapestry woven with threads of pain, joy, heartbreak, laughter—every emotion a brushstroke painting the portrait of my existence.

I find myself wondering about the paths untaken. What if I'd chosen to stay a devoted stay-at-home mom? How might my businesses have flourished if I'd been a more present mentor to my children? What if... The vision of being a grandparent once danced vividly in my mind. Dan and I would chuckle at the thought of surprising our adult children with tales of a Disney adventure with their own kids, while they stayed home lol. That dream, however, dimmed as we navigated the complex of our challenges. "Dan, I feel like a different person since the attack," I confess, my tears flowing freely. Dan's response is measured but knowing. "You might be, babe," he says, his gaze filled with understanding. He, too, bore the indelible marks of his own fateful day. Grand adventures with the little ones were now an impossibility, replaced by moments when even rising from bed felt like an immense feat for him. A weariness has settled into my bones. I long to bid farewell to the relentless hustle of life, to cast aside the weight of balancing budgets and scrutinizing spreadsheets that chart growth and setbacks. And then, there's the ache of feeling like I fell short in protecting Oliver. The attack on Oliver served as an unbidden reminder of our own mortality. The tears flow freely as I imagine my children facing the unimaginable loss of their mother in that terrifying moment. I can't help but feel a tinge of selfishness for saving Oliver, even as I am profoundly grateful for the outcome. In the midst of it all, one thing stands unwavering: unconditional love. It's the foundation upon which we rebuild our lives, a beacon of light guiding us through the darkest of days. Oliver, with his soulful eyes and wagging tail, embodies that love. He doesn't see the scars or the pain; he sees me, his human, imperfect but unwavering in my devotion. His presence is a calm to my wounded heart, a reminder that love transcends even the most harrowing of ordeals. Dan, too, personifies this boundless affection. He looks at me with eyes that hold no judgment, only compassion and a quiet understanding of the battles we've faced together. In his arms, I find solace, a sanctuary from the storm that rages within. It extends further, touching the lives of my children. They've witnessed their mother's strength and vulnerability, and in turn, they've shown me a love that knows no bounds. Their support, their unwavering belief in my resilience, they lift me when I feel like I might crumble. Sometimes, it's just a simple call, or text that shares a special moment of their lives with me. Unconditional love is the tapestry that weaves us all together, a force that mends the worn edges of our souls. It's in the moments we share, the laughter that punctuates our conversations, and the silent embraces that speak volumes. It's the legacy, it is my legacy. I want to leave behind—the knowledge that love, in all its forms, can conquer even the most difficult of challenges.

ABOUT THE AUTHOR

Melinda Small, author of "Finding Lindy," is a storyteller, entrepreneur, and advocate for personal growth. With a passion for connecting with others through narrative, Melinda draws on her own experiences to inspire and empower readers to embrace their own unique journey.

Born and raised in the small town of Millinocket, Maine, Melinda developed a deep appreciation for the power to overcome obstacles from a young age. As she navigates through life's challenges and triumphs, Melinda discovers the transformative power of resilience and self-discovery.

Melinda Small, happily married for 43 years, currently calls Minot, Maine, home. She remains dedicated to her passion for storytelling and personal growth, finding fulfillment in inspiring others along the way.